"The fact is that the average man's love of liberty is nine-tenths imaginary, exactly like his love of sense, justice and truth. He is not actually happy when free; he is uncomfortable, a bit alarmed, and intolerably lonely. Liberty is not a thing for the great masses of men. It is the exclusive possession of a small and disreputable minority, like knowledge, courage and honor. It takes a special sort of man to understand and enjoy liberty - and he is usually an outlaw in democratic societies."

H.L. Mencken, *Baltimore Evening Sun*, Feb. 12, 1923.

From SOVEREIGN to SERF

GOVERNMENT *by the* **TREACHERY**
and
DECEPTION *of* **WORDS**

by Roger S. Sayles

*When words lose their meaning,
the People lose their Liberty!* –

Confucius (551-479 B.C.)
(*The Analects*, XIII, 3)

Inspired by John Benson
Edited by Glenn Ambort
Cover by Kristi Kirk

© 2011 by Roger Sayles
All rights reserved.

All Rights Reserved. No part of this publication may be reproduced in any form or by any means, including scanning, photocopying, or otherwise without prior written permission of the copyright holder.

Disclaimer and Terms of Use: The Author and Publisher has strived to be as accurate and complete as possible in the creation of this book, notwithstanding the fact that he does not warrant or represent at any time that the contents within are accurate due to the rapidly changing nature of the Internet. While all attempts have been made to verify information provided in this publication, the Author and Publisher assumes no responsibility for errors, omissions, or contrary interpretation of the subject matter herein. Any perceived slights of specific persons, peoples, or organizations are unintentional. In practical advice books, Readers are cautioned to rely on their own judgment about their individual circumstances and to act accordingly. This book is not intended for use as a source of legal, business, accounting or financial advice. All readers are advised to seek services of competent professionals in legal, business, accounting, and finance fields.

Second Printing, 2012
Third Printing, 2013

Printed in the United States of America
ISBN 9781492708797

Contents

PROLOGUE ii

A BRIEF CHRONOLOGICAL HISTORY ... v

INTRODUCTION & FOREWORD xiii

PART I 1

PART II 25

PART III 61

APPENDIX 205

FOOTNOTES 211

BIOGRAPHY 219

~ PROLOGUE ~
The Advent of Modern, Voluntary Servitude in America Through Deceit and Deception

by David Straight

Roger Sayles and I have been friends for nearly 20 years. In several areas, we share a commonality of thoughts: offshore fishing and living free and responsibly.

He has asked me to write a prologue to his book—hoping that I could generalize a complex subject to make it easier for many readers to understand the specifics of what he has researched. It is a subject close to my heart, as I have read and researched for decades, seeking answers to the most important question that individuals should ask themselves. What is my status in society? Am I a slave, in servitude, or a free person whose body and assets are <u>not</u> <u>controlled</u> or <u>owned</u> by an outside force?

My father, born in 1908, was a self-taught historian, primarily of the Civil War and the Great Depression of the 1930s. While we were rebuilding the engine on my 1953 Ford Convertible Flat Head V8 in 1959, he explained to me the importance of understanding one's political status in society. He said it defined your relationship with your government – slave, serf or freeman. Are we private free citizens or public citizens, under the authority and jurisdiction (control) of the government? I told him that we were free citizens. He told me that was not true, that we were indeed second-class, federal citizens, who relinquished many of our liberties and constitutional rights. This was not the vision of our Forefathers. The gradual loss of our liberties and rights began after the Civil War and the ratification of the 14th Amendment, and accelerated during the Great Depression and bankruptcy of the United States in the 1930s. His words and well-articulated thoughts weighed heavily on my heart, for it demonstrates that our subjugation was brought about by means of a complex series of laws, policies and regulations shrouded in mystery and through which the American citizen voluntarily, but unwittingly, contracted to replace the status of free person with that of an inferior, or second-class, citizenship.

Roger's book sets forth several facts that you must fully grasp before you can appreciate the conclusions and remedies he presents therein:

1.) Over time, the Federal Government has gradually usurped most of the power constitutionally granted to the states.

- State primacy became Federal primacy.

- State citizenship was usurped by the Federal Government, which thereupon established the U.S. citizen as a 2nd class citizen (public citizen).

<u>This Is the Big One</u>

- Americans unwittingly, supposedly voluntarily, accepted Federal or U.S. Government jurisdiction over their lives by <u>declaring</u> that they were <u>U.S. citizens</u>.

    o We declare it for our children on the birth certificate;

    o We declare it when we file our taxes;

    o We declare it on our passports, bank accounts etc.

2.) When you declare yourself to be a U.S. citizen, you contract and enter into the legal status of second-class citizenship. Once you have contracted into this inferior, second-class U.S. citizenship, you become subject to many regulations, policies and laws, including their many onerous duties and responsibilities, most of which could not be applied to State citizens simply because, under the Constitution, as it existed before ratification of the 14th Amendment, the Federal Government lacked the constitutional jurisdiction to reach

State citizens, except under limited and enumerated powers delegated to it by the several States of the Union. As you will learn, the 14th Amendment gave the Federal Government virtually unlimited powers and jurisdiction over its newly-created second-class U.S. citizens.

There are three extremely important legal and political verbal landmines that you must learn about on the road to freedom: the new U.S. citizen and resident (not a geographical, but a political term) created by the 14th Amendment and the new federal jurisdiction, meaning legal control or power, brought into existence by that Amendment. These three terms lie at the very heart of the Federal Government's introduction of the feudal law into our Nation, the very same feudal law that our Forebears had shed their blood to banish forever from this Land and from their posterity.

The facts, law and history presented to you will leave many people in a state of incredulity, others will be outraged and a few will dismiss them outright. However, they do demonstrate that "We Americans," in direct conflict with our American Heritage and beliefs, have existed for decades in a form of bondage that is foreign to the American way of life and a violation of the sense of freedom that exists in the hearts and souls of Americans. We're right back to the situation that faced our Forebears, when Thomas Jefferson stated in the Declaration of Independence, speaking of King George III of England:

> *He has combined with others to subject us to a jurisdiction foreign to our constitution, and unacknowledged by our laws.*

Isn't the feudal-law jurisdiction imposed upon us today foreign to our Constitution?

How our modern rulers have combined with others (international bankers, etc.?) to subject us to a jurisdiction foreign to our Constitution is a mystery and deception that requires unraveling before we move farther and farther away from the dream and commitment of our Forefathers who mutually pledged to each other their lives, their fortunes and their sacred honor to make America "The Land of The Free."

How you react to this information will be a matter of how strongly it touches your heart and soul. Of equal importance, how willing are you to learn correctly how to claim your new citizen status and remove yourself from the jurisdiction of a government that guards its power jealously and seriously?

However, knowledge in itself is power, and there is power in numbers. In the end, even the most powerful governments fail when facing the wrath of the people.

I'm certain there are many Americans who would knowingly choose to be Federal citizens (U.S. citizen) to receive the myriad of protective benefits in exchange for their freedoms. I believe many more would not, <u>if offered the choice</u>.

Personally, I cherish the restrictions placed on our Federal Government by the Constitution of the United States of America. My spirit demands the protection of that glorious instrument granted to Americans. I abhor any form of bondage.

I believe that we Americans have volunteered, unwittingly, into federal bondage and that a fraud has been perpetrated that *must* be addressed. The fraud lies in the execution of a contract without knowledge of its intent.

A Brief Chronological History, More Clearly Defined by Roger Sayles

Following the U.S. Civil War, the Federal Government established its primacy over the individual States and commenced its expanding and relentless quest to establish, through law and deception, a new class of citizen which would "voluntarily" relinquish its rights and power to a federal authority that would then assume jurisdiction and control over its citizens, their bodies and their assets.

Certainly, history has proven that to be a fact, for good or for ill, and the question of individual States Rights appears to have been settled by that war. As a result of the Union victory in the Civil War, the states lost their right to secede, a right many felt was part of the original intent of the Founders of the Constitution. With the passage of the 13th Amendment to the Constitution in 1865, involuntary servitude (slavery) was outlawed in the United States. The 13th Amendment created a complex legal problem. Unlike the Citizens of the States, the free slaves, then known as 'Freedmen,' had no legal or political protection. They had no political status. To solve the dilemma, a new status of U.S. citizen was established by the 14th Amendment of the Constitution – a federal or 2nd class citizen, a public, not a private, citizen.

For moral and legal reasons, the free slaves were granted citizenship with the ability to enjoy any of the privileges and immunities of Federal citizenship, but through the act of the law, these citizens were "subject to the jurisdiction (control and protection) of the Federal United States." Hence, the former slaves became Federal citizens via the 14th Amendment, but, as the Supreme Court later ruled, did not possess the free status and God-given rights of the natural-born U.S. State citizens.

This is an extremely important point to remember and consider. Why? Because, over time and through deceptive legal maneuvering, the inferior or 2nd class Federal citizenship was ascribed to all natural-born Americans, who had, our government agents tell us, voluntarily entered into this second-class status, even though most, if not all, had done so unknowingly. It is a mystery to me, perhaps to you, too, how one can make a voluntary choice between alternative courses of action open to him or her, if one is unaware of those alternatives.

~ Recap ~

Since we have supposedly volunteered into a 2nd class status (Resident U.S. citizen), we have placed ourselves under the feudal-law jurisdiction of the Federal Government, thereby relinquishing many of our natural or God-given rights, as well as the constitutional protections thereof.

We are modern-day, medieval serfs, far more valuable to those in power than a plantation slave. Why? The modern day 2nd class U.S. citizen manages his own life, believes that he is free, though our body, our assets and our property are owned and pledged to the Federal Government and the central banking system, the Federal Reserve. The medieval serf knew and understood his status in society. We Americans are totally ignorant of our true status as serfs on the Federal Manor.

The U.S. State Department addresses all issues of citizenship. Few Americans are aware that two forms of citizenship exist in The United States.

- One is the Resident U.S. citizen, which represents over 95% of Americans. All individuals in America who declare themselves to be U.S. citizens declare, in effect, that they voluntarily place themselves under the feudal-law jurisdiction (control) of the Federal Government and pledge their bodies, assets and labor to the federal authority – 2nd class citizens (serfs).

- The other is the U.S. National.

What is the difference between these two citizenship statuses? Is there a manner in which a U.S. citizen can change his status through a legal declaration?

That is the purpose of Roger's book. It contains a chronological history of the events and law which have placed once-free, private individuals under the control or feudal jurisdiction of the Federal Government and who are, today, called public, federal or U.S. citizens.

The limitations placed on the Federal Government by the Constitution and the protections it guarantees to Americans do not necessarily apply to U.S. citizen residents. They will apply only if there is a loud, vocal outcry from the populace, a

cry which will eventually be heard by the U.S. Supreme Court, which will then be compelled to uphold these limitations and protections. Such cries will never reach the High Court unless We, the People, are educated about such limitations and protections and demand that they be respected.

However, like all magicians, the political wizards behind our national scenes are loath to show their hands lest their "mystery" should unravel and the people go free.

As Dr. Adam Weishaupt stated, *"Of all the means I know to lead men, the most effective is concealed mystery."* Very few Americans understand why the protections granted to Americans under our U.S. Constitution appear to have little consequence in today's society. Certainly, the laws, regulations and policies implemented have long demonstrated that constitutional protections do *not* exist in our status of 2nd class, public, Federal U. S. citizens.

~ A Recent Example ~

In June of 2011, the Indiana Supreme Court, in a ruling on domestic violence, stated that Hoosier residents have no right to resist unlawful police entry into their home, in violation of the 4th Amendment of our Constitution, which prohibits illegal search and seizure without probable cause, etc. I believe this ruling, under which our home is no longer our castle, will ultimately be struck down by the U.S. Supreme Court, not to protect the U.S. citizens, but to demonstrate its role as the primary government force and to help maintain the illusion that the Constitution is the "Supreme Law of the Land" – at least for the few who are not U.S. citizens.

Today, constitutional rights or issues are seldom considered but are replaced by "public policy" and Civil Law, to which we U.S. citizens voluntarily agree, supposedly, when we place ourselves under the feudal jurisdiction (control) of the Federal Government.

Does this concern you? If not, they win, we lose! It definitely concerns me!

Honestly, what does it take for "We Americans" to wake up and demand or declare our God-given rights and constitutional protections?

Restrictions of the powers of all governments: *Shall not disable any <u>natural</u> or <u>constitutional</u> right without due process of law, and then only to the extent necessary to avoid infringing the rights of others.*

Could any cognizant American deny that rulings such as that of the Indiana Supreme Court, like the rulings of many other courts, demonstrate that those who make and interpret our laws have little regard for their oaths to preserve, protect, and defend our U.S. Constitution? Perhaps it is irrelevant due to our diminished status.

One must consider the ruling by the Supreme Court of the United States in the *Slaughter-House* Cases (1873*)*, which has never been refuted or challenged. The case involved state citizens from Louisiana who were seeking relief from the federal jurisdiction on a state issue. The Federal Supreme Court reaffirmed the primacy of the state <u>and</u> the privileges and immunities of the natural born <u>citizen</u> <u>of</u> <u>the</u> <u>state</u>, not the 14th Amendment Federal citizen. The private state citizens were sent packing back to their state for relief. That process would be reversed today, as we are federal citizens (U.S. citizens). Here's what the Court said:

> *Of the privileges and immunities of the citizens of the United States and of the privileges and immunities of the citizens of a state...<u>it is only the former which is placed by the clause (the second clause of the 14th Amendment) under the protection of the Federal Constitution</u>, and that*
>
> *the latter, whatever they may be, are not intended to have any additional protection by this paragraph*

> *of the Amendment...the latter must rest for their security and protection where they have heretofore rested, for they are not embraced by this paragraph of the Amendment...*
>
> *But with...exceptions...few...the entire domain of the privileges and immunities of citizens of the state, as above defined, <u>lay within the constitutional and legislative power of the state and without that of the Federal Government</u>. Was it the purpose of the 14th Amendment...to transfer the security and protection of all the civil rights which we have mentioned from the states to the Federal Government? And . . . was it intended to bring within the power of Congress the entire domain of civil rights heretofore belonging exclusively to the States?* [No! my comment.]

For legal remedy, state citizens, with few exceptions, worked within the state where they lived, as the Federal Government had no jurisdiction over the state citizen or state issues. Its jurisdiction was over the 14th Amendment federal citizen, and that citizenship was limited to the slaves who had been freed by the 13th Amendment.

All governments evolve. Representative republics, such as ours, which restrict federal power, become democracies (rule of the majority), then socialistic and, history demonstrates, ultimately fail. The average republic exists for 200 years. At the time of its failure, it looks nothing like the original protective contract executed by the states / people. This is an historical, empirical truth. The reasons are legion, often related to power and the demands of the populace for security and protection. Initially the changes will be small, and then they begin to pile up, layer upon layer, until there is a tipping point, from which the populace / citizens awaken and find themselves enslaved by the government designed by contract to preserve and protect them within specific limitations.

Because we live in a country bound by laws, there seems to be only one logical, legal maneuver which would allow such apparent violations of our Constitutional Rights and immunities to come about: somehow persuade the citizens to place themselves under the jurisdiction (control) of the U.S. Federal Government – <u>voluntarily</u> but without actual knowledge of the precious gift relinquished thereby.

So strap on your seatbelt and be sure to cruise slowly through the following text. You volunteered yourself into this mess. Now let Roger show you how to volunteer yourself out.

David Straight, 2011

David Straight resides in north Georgia. He is a father, a grandfather and a committed hard worker that made him a millionaire at a relatively young age. Prior to that he served in Vietnam with the U. S. Naval Air and still holds fast to the oath he took. In the 1990s, he spent much of his spare time promoting a nationally successful program called "Liberty Bell" and another in which he outlined how counties could reaffirm the constitution as the supreme law of the land. He got the law passed in his home county and others.

In Memorium; David Straight

As one gets older some of life's ironies and involvements seem to come 'full circle.' This is one of those instances.

One of the dearest friends I have had in this life, one of the men who crossed my path that I liked, admired and respected the most was David Straight. The irony of the situation is that David and I initially met and became such good and close friends all these years due to the information contained in this book. David was invited to one of the early presentations I gave for several years in the Atlanta area concerning the topics covered between the following pages. We did not have the total picture in those years. We only understood the tax side of the equation, not the total jurisdictional picture we have now. David and I would spend countless hours discussing and debating these points and issues the remaining 17 plus years we were friends and, I should say, 'brothers in arms' in the animated fight for knowledge, understanding and liberty.

My dear, old and trusted friend David Straight went to his great reward quietly and peacefully in his sleep on May 8, 2012 shortly after turning 69. Rest in peace dear friend. I dearly miss your 'wise council.' I am so very honored that you wrote the Forward to this powerful work. May your words be a tribute to your spirit, knowledge, understanding, compassion and honor. A finer man I have never met.

Roger S. Sayles
August 2012

~ Introduction & Foreword~

This book is about words. The only appropriate way to begin this study and dissection of words is by making the following personal statement:

Words cannot express my gratitude to you, not only for purchasing this book, but also for having the drive and courage to seek the truth about a world that is currently swirling out of control around all of us, no matter where we are located on the globe. The world today has been taken over and is effectively controlled by those individuals who have spawned and mastered the deceitful and evil usage of words, resulting in mass confusion and chaos all around us. Like any other tool, words can be used for good or for evil. It is my heartfelt hope and prayer that, in your quest to find, and hopefully live, the truth, you will be able to reach some semblance of your full God-given potential. This can be accomplished by using words to your advantage based upon knowledge and understanding. With your increased knowledge and understanding, our traditional and timeless enemy can have his most important weapon of carnage, destruction and control turned and used against him. This will not come automatically, just by reading; it will take some time, effort and study on your part.

We have been told that we should develop the talents we have each been given. The information presented here has given me that path to walk for 18.5 years at this point in my life. By walking this long, arduous and often frustrating path, I have come to realize many things, not only about myself, but also about the world and life as our Creator meant it to be lived. These ideas and ideals are about how life should be lived not only personally but also in relation to others. It has, as of today, made me the best and most effective and complete person I have ever been in my almost 63 years. I hope I can pass the baton of truth on to you so that you can run your own personal leg of this challenging race. I can neither run your race for you nor help you fulfill your destiny; that is your job and mandate. All I can do is help awaken the true spirit of truth and liberty that I believe lies deep in each and every one of our hearts and burns deeply within our breasts. Not everyone has that flame that burns as intensely as it does within me. I have learned this through many painful experiences. However, the fact that you have somehow heard the message and been motivated to possess and read this book tells me that you may be one who also has that unquenchable desire to seek, know and understand truth.

As I write these words, it is the afternoon of April 14, 2011, just one day before tax day in the United States. It is a spectacularly beautiful fall day in Argentina, a country I now call home. As I write, literal tears of gratitude pour from my eyes. They are heartfelt and sincere. This project has been my life's major goal for the last 18 years. I think I must be one of the rare and fortunate men in history who are given the opportunity not only to know, but also to realize and accomplish their life's major goal. The feelings of accomplishment and fulfillment that come from being able to reach this goal burn hot and deep within my breast. They are feelings and emotions that I am unable to express in mere words. My gratitude is boundless and my humility heartfelt and sincere.

I cannot write further without giving the appropriate credit and thanks to those who have shown and helped me walk this long, often frustrating and rewarding path. First of all my love, thanks and gratitude go to our Creator, the Mighty Jehovah. It is He who puts the burning desire for freedom in our collective breasts and hearts. It is He who has given me the inspiration, drive, determination and stamina to get to this point in my personal journey. It is from Him that I derive my strength, resolve and determination. For it was through the knowledge and understanding contained in these pages that I found Him.

I say this because I did not find God directly, as many do. I found God and know beyond a shadow of a doubt that He exists only because of this information and the growth it allowed me to have. I offer this as my personal testimony. All I can do is to present and attempt to teach you what I have learned and explain the path I have walked. As each and every of the many teachers I had along the way told me, *"This is a spiritual battle."* Initially, that statement confused me; I did not fully comprehend or understand it. However, after a few years, the fog lifted and the curtain was drawn aside. This IS a 'spiritual battle' and, like it or not, a battle in which each of us is, or soon will be, heavily engaged. It is the ancient and timeless battle of good versus evil. It is my fondest hope and most fervent desire that the information and truths contained herein will help you discern the part you are meant to play in this eternal struggle for truth and freedom.

To those who crossed my path, certainly by NO accident, in July of 1992, I give my deepest and most sincere gratitude. John Benson and Glenn Ambort. The dedication of these two men, regardless of the consequences they suffered and endured, humble me and give me an example not only to emulate, but also to follow. I consider John Benson to be the single greatest man that has ever crossed my life's path. He is, and has been, like a father to me in many ways. The knowledge he has absorbed and attained still boggles my conscious thoughts. John is a man who has given his entire adult life to discovering the facts contained herein and teaching them to others like me. It is, without a doubt, his destiny. You are being exposed to his knowledge and life's work by reading this small book. You are helping him and me fulfill our mutual destinies. I salute John, as I'm certain you will after you have digested the truths within this book. John is the source; I am his messenger as I now pass these truths herein. It is my sincere prayer that they will have a similarly profound effect on you as they have had upon me.

John Benson went to great lengths and much personal sacrifice to uncover the legal concepts and facts presented herein. For example, he lived in a warehouse for over 16 months to save on expenses and so that he had the time to do the needed legal research. During this time John slept on a mattress on a concrete floor when he wasn't reading court cases and law books. Already in poor health and suffering from cataracts in both eyes, he read cases with a magnifying glass as thick as the bottom of a Coke bottle. He did this so that you would be able to read and internalize this valuable information. John would often repeat in those long seminars, "the ONLY WAY I can protect my liberty is to help you protect yours!" Now it's your turn to learn about, gain and protect your God-given freedoms and liberties. These are the precious freedoms for which our Forebears gave their lives, fortunes and sacred honor. Those brave men and women gave their all. Most of them died penniless and destitute for their efforts. What are YOU willing to sacrifice?

The second person I want to acknowledge at this point is Glenn Ambort. Glenn has been "the spark-plug" that drives the freedom engine; John's contribution was the gas. As I write this, Glenn has recently been released after serving 8 ½ years of a 9 year sentence in federal prison for simply daring to teach what you are about to read and, I hope, study and internalize. John was released in July of 2008. Glenn is currently in a subsidized apartment for homeless veterans as he re-enters society or at least what is left of the society he was forcibly removed from! Glenn is an Annapolis graduate and a Navy and Marine Corps veteran. What I am going to tell you next was not told to me by him; he's much too humble for that. In fact I do not know that he even knows that I know this part of his younger life, as I have never personally discussed it with him. A mutual friend of ours, and a classmate of Glenn's at Annapolis, the U.S. Naval Academy, is the one who related this information to me.

While Glenn was at the Naval Academy, the Academy was fortunate enough to have a young star football quarterback enrolled also. The military academies' main curriculum, if I understand it correctly, is military engineering. Not exactly an easy subject matter for most people. Glenn helped the young football quarterback by helping him with his academic subjects on occasion. This enabled him to receive not only his degree from the Naval Academy but he also won the Heisman Trophy. That young quarterback is one of only two Academy graduates ever to win the Heisman Trophy. He went on to have a brilliant and storied career as the quarterback of "America's Team," the Dallas Cowboys. His name is Roger Staubach. Glenn has been a true inspiration, guide and example for me during these last 18 1/2 years. Obviously he has been an inspiration to others also. Glenn, I salute you for your work, dedication and sacrifice and for being who you are!

Many other people in the Atlanta area and all over our great country have contributed to my success along the way. It would be impossible to name them all here. Those of you reading these words know exactly who you are and realize, I hope, the size and impact of your contribution.

This book is written in two parts. The reason for this is the tragic events on September 11, 2001. After years of trying to tell/teach people these concepts and mostly having them fall on deaf ears, I came to the realization that the American people were not ready to listen. It seemed to me that I was just beating my head against the wall because it felt so damn good when I stopped! At that point, I put down my teaching efforts and concentrated on living my life by the principles and truths that I had learned and come to realize. Those are mostly contained herein. It would take a book of many pages to pass them all along to you. And honestly, I do not know that even today I have come to realize them all yet. I have tried my best to cover the most important ones.

After 9/11 became exposed and questioned by a large segment of the country in 2005, I felt that many people were beginning to listen. That is when Part II of this book was originally written. I had moved physical locations twice by then and much of the material was scattered. It had to be reassembled and organized. Much of what you will read had to be hand-typed. I spent many, many hours on this project as a "labor of love." At that point, I took the still-rough first draft and sent it to practically every major patriot talk show host in the country. Even after phone calls to several of them with whom I had personal relationships, I still got no response.

It was only a few years after that time that I felt like I was being guided to move out of the United States and leave the country of my birth. I no longer call the U.S. "my country" but "the country of my birth." The reason I have taken this stance is that I came to realize that America is not just a country; it is a unique gathering of principles and ideals. It is not just a landmass contained within defined borders. You can easily read those principles and ideals in its founding documents along with the eloquent and insightful writings of the Founding Fathers. It is easy to see that they were highly educated men with great moral fiber, character and courage. America was based on timeless and immutable principles, high ideals, morals and ethics. The United States Government no longer embodies those concepts. A country operating under those concepts does not go around the world making war, taking over other countries in order to control their resources and killing women and children. Unable to effect a change from within, I voted with my feet! I now feel that I may be able to bring about change for the Nation and People whom I love, but from without.

With the passage and implementation of the Patriot Act, I was feeling more and more restricted in the lifestyle I had chosen to lead. Please, understand that I was, and have been since December 31, 1992, a true free man. I was a free man, by law, living in a land of slaves who THINK they are free men! Johann Wolfgang von Goethe stated it well, "There are none so helplessly enslaved as those who falsely believe they are free." His quote came to mind often when I spoke to the majority of people at that time. That wasn't my only reason for wanting to leave the country and relocate but, it was certainly one of the main ones. That was when, I will always believe, God showed me a television program on one Saturday night about Argentina.

I had a dear 35-year friend, since deceased, who had purchased property here several years before. He kept trying to get me down to Argentina for a visit with him on one of his many trips dealing with the property he had purchased. At that point I did not have nor had I ever had the need to have a passport. The decision to leave and being required to apply for and receive a passport are, I will always believe, the main reasons behind my writing what you are reading today. For, it was in the first 30 seconds of reading the application, in the WARNING box, that all of the knowledge and understanding that I had spent years acquiring and constantly pondering came to an apex. It was one of those rare and magic moments in life when things just come into focus. Now I recognized beyond any doubt what the other form of political status that I had long-before acquired was, but had never been able to correctly identify. It was set forth in that warning box so clearly by the very officials who practice the tyranny of words, but was clear to me only because my previous training and thought had prepared me to see it and comprehend it. Earlier, in 1992 or 1993, I had been told by the Florida Attorney General that "all matters of citizenship are decided by the U.S. Department of State." As the passport application is an "official document" of the State Department (often referred to as "foggy bottom"), I knew I had found an important source document and an integral missing part of the government's word-game puzzle. As I read further into that federal passport application and got to the 'oath,' I knew I had them! That passport application had presented me a means by which to teach this complicated legal information without going through two hours of tedious, complicated legal information to prove to anyone that would listen that there are two distinct and different types of political status, citizenship if you will, in the United States. That application gave me an official document by which to show to anyone, who is willing to listen and think 'outside the box,' the method used by the federal government to deceive its own people.

Part I of this book was written over the first few weeks in April of 2011. Rather than attempt to incorporate it within the body of the previous work, I have decided to present it in two different parts. Hopefully the proofs in Part I will give you a quicker and better understanding and insight into reading and understanding the facts and case for freedom presented in Part II.

This information gives the clearest crosscut view of your enemy and his tactics that I have ever seen, found or heard. I want you to fully comprehend that those who would deceive you had to reach deep down into their bag of tricks to take over the freest country in the history of the world and turn it into a land of confused legal slaves.

The United States is only the second country in history where man has been able to receive God-given, Natural Rights. We have been collectively tricked out of those Rights and been placed into the legal status of bondage and slavery. Legally, you are merely an asset owned or pledged by the federal government. International bankers own and control you and those whom you love as pieces of property to be used, bartered, bought and sold as collateral in their bogus paper money schemes! If that doesn't make you mad or send chills up your spine, you may not be the person who is supposed to be reading this. If you are not driven to learn and understand what has been done to us in this dreadful scheme, you may not be the person who is supposed to be exposed to this book and the information herein.

It is said that *"the truth shall set you free."* Within these pages you will be exposed to truth. You will be exposed to the truth like you have never been exposed to it before, I dare say, in your entire life. You will be exposed to established legal concepts that date back to Rome. You will read excerpts from decisions handed down by the United States Supreme Court, some cases decided over 100 years ago, that remain good law today. They have never been overturned or overruled. These are FACTS, not theories such as you hear many stating publicly today. What you do with it now and in our collective futures is entirely up to you. "Many are called, few are chosen."

May God guide you and walk by your side in this great endeavor to speak truth to those who occupy the seats of power!

Sincerely,

Roger S. Sayles

Part I

"I believe that it is better to tell the truth than a lie. I believe it is better to be free than to be a slave. And I believe it is better to know than to be ignorant." - H.L. Mencken

"Words mean things!" That was a Rush Limbaugh mantra in the early days of his highly successful syndicated radio show. These days, I and millions of others have ceased listening to his 'left-right paradigm prop-agenda.' I do not think that he uses that phrase anymore. However, that does not minimize the truth behind that saying. "Words do mean things," as we shall see very clearly and dramatically in the pages that follow. I have 'turned a phrase' here as the saying goes: *"Sticks and stones can break my bones but words can never hurt me"* was an old saying we should all remember. The remaining topics and subjects in this book come under the turned phrase.

> ***"Sticks and stones can break my bones but words can, and have, enslaved me!"***

"Words mean things" to the federal government also. The trick is to understand the definition that is being given or implied by the context in which those words are being used. This is the key to the "big secret." The "big secret" is that we have been enslaved and totally controlled by a network of regulatory agencies. They have achieved this through the treachery of words that have been used to trick our minds. The real "big secret" is exactly HOW that is being/has been done. I am now going to demonstrate this treachery to you now by using the single most important information-gathering form used by the federal government to determine your political and civil status. This single form allows you to inform the government of the nature of your national citizenship. Remember what I was told by the Florida Attorney General, "ALL matters having to do with citizenship are decided by the U.S. Department of State."

After we have seen that we will, to the extent the length of this book allows, explore exactly how an entire nation of free men and women have been converted to federal feudal slaves under the exact same form of slavery that governed most of Europe and England for almost 1,000 years. For years, people have said "there are two sets of laws, one for them and one for us." That is true. Today, I'm going to show them to you from the U.S. Department of State's official form!

For over 18 years I have been trying to teach people these facts and this information from the "bottom up," by learning the basics of laws that have since ceased being taught at most, if not all, law schools. Now we have found the perfect document, printed by the Government Printing Office that will illustrate what has been done from the "top down" approach.

This form can be found at:
http://www.state.gov/documents/organization/79960.pdf.

This is the **Renewal Passport Application** from the U.S. Department of State. For one's initial application, there is a separate application. They are both basically the same. Or you can put "U.S. Passport Application" in any internet search engine to obtain either or both forms. Curious already?

If you do not have immediate access to the Internet, you can simply drop by any United States Post Office and request either an original, first-time application or a renewal hard copy of this document. You may want to pick up both forms.

As I was told in a letter from the State of Florida Attorney General's office when I wrote, early on in my awakening and education, asking for some sort of State certificate stating that I was a citizen of the State of Florida, "*__ALL matters of citizenship are handled by the U.S. Department of State.__*" This passport application is the U.S. Department of State's form and is under its total jurisdiction, at least according to the Attorney General of the State of Florida.

It is important to understand that a U.S. Passport is the single most important document in the entire arsenal of federal government identification documents. It serves not only to identify you, but also to set forth your legal status and personality. This document is used to identify you not only within the United States (of America) but also outside our great country anywhere in the world. This passport application, therefore, by logic and deduction, automatically becomes the most important application for receipt of this extremely important identifying document. As there are two distinct legal statuses listed, it also becomes an important document in designating your true and correct political status.

The first thing I want to bring to your attention is the 'black boxed' statement at the bottom of page 1 with the bold, capital letters **"WARNING."** In the original forms from the U.S. Post Office this is 'not' boxed but located at the top of either form. From looking at both original and reapplication forms from the Post Office, it is apparent that in the original (orange color scheme in the copies I currently possess) application, the lettering is in a 'very small' font. In the reapplication form (purple color scheme), it is printed in a much larger font although the rest of the body of the application appears to be the same.

Please notice the positioning of this black-boxed "WARNING" in the Internet application of the entire document. It is located on the first page buried in the instructions. Pay close attention to the specific wording, especially the phrase "Affidavit or other supporting documents submitted therewith." On the original forms from the Post Office it is located at the top of the document. In fact, it is the first body of instructions that one reads when reading either hard copy application.

Read this section closely, to wit:

> "*WARNING*: *False statements made knowingly and willfully in passport applications including affidavits or other supporting documents submitted therewith, are punishable by fine and/or imprisonment under the provisions of 18 U.S.C., [et seq]......... All statements and documents are subject to verification.*"

It is important to note that you can submit different types of declarations or documents with your application, "including Affidavits." The documentation that you submit can be attached to and made a part of your application simply by its inclusion in the process.

Notice that they do not state any particular reason that such documentation could, or even more specifically, 'should' be attached. The creators of this form merely note that, if there are any 'false statements' made in such documentation, you face the possibility of some sort of fine or even imprisonment. Isn't it unfortunate that federal government officials or agents can't be held to such a high standard?

Now, jump ahead to the actual application itself. Go to the bottom of the second page of the actual application and find the "Oath." Many Americans feel that some, perhaps many, federal officials and agents do not consider any oath they take very seriously.

However, we do know that any oath that YOU make is taken VERY seriously by government officials. For instance, the phrase "under penalty of perjury" appears above your signature at the bottom of a 1040 Tax Form and is taken very seriously by the IRS.

Here is the exact statement/oath, numbered section #23, in the orange color-scheme hard copy I have currently in front of me in the middle of page 2 of 2.

> "*__I declare under penalty of perjury that I am a United States citizen (or non- citizen national) and have not, since acquiring United States citizenship (or U.S. nationality), performed any of the acts listed under "Acts or Conditions" on the reverse of this application form (unless explanatory statement is attached). I declare under penalty of perjury that the statements made on this application are true and correct__*."

__Above the oath, in large, bold lettering, is the word "STOP!" It is followed (also in bold caps) by this warning:__

> "*__DO NOT SIG APPLICATION UNTIL REQUESTED TO DO SO BY PERSON ADMINISTERING OATH__*."

__Obviously they take this oath quite seriously. So should you!__

Note that there are TWO DIFFERENT AND DISTINCT types of legal statuses in the United States. The first is a "citizen of the United States." The second is a "__NON- CITIZEN national of the United States.__" Please understand that these two are mutually exclusive hence the "**NON-CITIZEN**" designation. These two are totally separate legal personalities and distinct from each other as specified by the government's own specific instructions and detailed wording in this important passport application document.

Elsewhere in the instructions for application, it is plainly stated on the first page. The two statuses are once again separate and in capital letters:

> *"US PASSPORTS ARE ISSUED ONLY TO US CITIZENS OR NON-CITIZEN NATIONALS. EACH PERSON MUST OBTAIN HIS OR HER OWN PASSPORT."*

They emphasize throughout the entire document and the instructions thereto that there are two separate and distinct types of legal statuses and personalities. The two statuses are also mentioned in at least one other part of the instructions for the application.

Also, under the heading PAPERWORK REDUCTION STATEMENT appears the following:

> *"You are not required to provide the information requested on this form unless the form displays a currently valid OMB number. We try to create forms and instructions that can be easily understood. **OFTEN THIS IS DIFFICULT TO DO BECAUSE OUR CITIZENSHIP LAWS ARE VERY COMPLEX**.*"(Bold and caps added by me.)

That statement has to be one of the greatest understatements you will ever see in print in any federal government form. Explaining those "complex citizenship laws" is the major purpose of this small, telling and revealing book! It is also the reason that my mentors, John Benson and Glenn Ambort, have collectively spent 14 years in Club Fed! For 'some mysterious reason,' the U.S. Department of Just-US did not want them to expose this to the people or, more appropriately, the feudal slaves.

Now, take a good look at the ending of the first sentence in the oath. There it is stated that, if you have performed any of the "Acts or Conditions" listed on the reverse side of the application, you must attach an explanation. It is clearly stated, "**unless explanatory statement is attached.**"

Why is it that the federal government would NOT ask you to attach a "statement" explaining which of the two legal statuses applies to you? Why does the form not ask you clearly to add documentation concerning your status as a U.S. citizen (or non-citizen national) in the oath? Why does the form mention the two different statuses at the very top of the form where the average person would not be inclined to question it? Why would they also threaten an applicant with such severe potential penalties? I feel certain that, in the vast majority of cases, one would never even question which of the two statuses applied to him or her, much less put two and two together. Do I have to spell out the answer any more clearly?

A 'person' (another word of legal art) can ONLY get Rights from one of two ways. You can acquire your Rights the way our Founders felt they acquired theirs from Nature and Nature's God. Notice in the founding documents the capital "R." The ONLY OTHER way you can get rights is from man. These may be called rights but they are actually privileges. Privileges are given by man and can easily be altered, changed or taken away entirely by man. These privileges, now called "civil rights," have replaced your God-given Rights. This was accomplished by your unconscious act of literally, legally, asking for them. When asked "are you a citizen of the United States?" or "are you a resident?" you answered "yes." Our rulers have thus allowed you to be tricked into 'volunteering' into a special and specific political status where you have been given privileges called "civil rights" which automatically replaced your Natural God-given Rights.

Do you see and understand their tactics here? Under our system of law, "Ignorance of the law is no excuse." Our government officials do not have to tell you that you are being enslaved or that you were 'volunteering' to be a slave. They simply asked you what status you were in a very deceitful manner, utilizing a legally presumptive, and leading question. You, having been tricked by the words, told them exactly what they wanted to hear: "Yes, I am one of the serfs on the federal feudal manor!" Tyranny exists when someone 'tells' you that you are a slave. They did not tell you that you were a slave; they asked you and you answered! You should know what you are, shouldn't you? "Ignorance of the law" notwithstanding! Now do you understand the tactics here a little more clearly? If not, you do not know your enemy very well, yet! You will, as you continue reading and learning.

So, it should be very plain that, at least according to U.S. federal government terminology (and we know they are 'always' correct, aren't they) that there are two distinct and different types of 'persons,' entirely different from each other, and with two separate and distinct legal personalities. One is called a "citizen of the United States" and has civil rights (small 'r'), actually privileges, under the scope and purview of the 14th Amendment to the U.S. Constitution. (More about this later.) The other, a "non-citizen U.S.

national," is the legal person who has God-given, Constitutionally-protected, Natural Rights. Many people erroneously refer to these as "Constitutional Rights." That is incorrect! They are God-Given and Constitutionally-PROTECTED! Those are the Rights that were defined by Thomas Jefferson in the opening lines of the second paragraph of the Declaration of Independence. Those lines are:

> *"We hold these Truths to be self –evident, that all Men are created equal, that they are endowed by their Creator with certain unalienable Rights, that among these are Life, Liberty, and the Pursuit of Happiness…"*

The sometimes-confusing word "Happiness" was substituted for the word "Property" in the original draft. Which political status defines you? Which "person" are you? Only YOU can decide that. The roadmap to acquiring that status, the one you have been tricked out of, is contained in this relatively small, but extremely "illuminating" (pun intended), and important writing.

In this first part of the book are the things that have come, or 'occurred,' to me over the last six years after the main part, Part II, was written. I will now move to the second big realization that has come to me, at least as it pertains to being able to relatively easily frame things in a way that is more understandable for someone trying to "untie the knots" that have been placed in our collective minds. A BIG key to being able to understand this dreadful scheme is understanding the Administrative or Regulatory Agencies. Not only to understand them and how they were designed and work, but exactly where they fit into this system of slavery that has been placed over the American people. This also encompasses how to avoid giving them facts or reasons to justify their jurisdiction over you. For, if they have no jurisdiction over you, you should not have to interact with them at all. If you think about it seriously, you'll realize that the officials in these agencies are the ones that ALWAYS come after you. As one of my legal teachers kept telling me, "they're the ones that ding you!" I will do my very best to attempt to explain them in the most simplistic terms possible.

Administrative, or Regulatory, Agencies came into the American political organizational chart mainly during the 1930s; many more have been added since. They have proliferated and increased in number and have become considerably more brazen in their actions and enforcement. They were originally spawned during the Great Depression, after the bankruptcy of the United States of America and the confiscation of the American people's wealth (the gold confiscation in April, 1933). It was during this era that the country was put into literal 'receivership' of the International Monetary Fund. It was during this time-frame that Congressman Louis T. McFadden made this very telling and prophetic statement on the floor of the U.S. House of Representatives:

> *"The 'new-deal' lawyers now have no hesitancy in appearing in court and asserting that private citizens can contract away their constitutional rights."*

How this was done is covered in much greater detail in the following pages.

The law that outlines the powers, duties and responsibilities, of regulatory agencies, along with exactly how they are required to administer and regulate their subject-matter, are covered in the Administrative Procedures Act. Passage of this piece of governing legislation was attempted several times over much of the latter part of the 1930s but was never passed and signed into law. It was finally passed as law, and incorporated in the U.S. Statutes (Title 5, U.S. Code) in 1946 after the second great banker's war. The APA, as it's referred to, lays out all of the legal requirements that must be strictly adhered to by these newly formed federal agencies designed to regulate and govern their slaves who had, as McFadden stated above, been tricked into signing away their God-given, Constitutionally-protected Rights in exchange for federal privileges called "civil rights." The first thing we need to cover is the method by which laws are written and promulgated (put into effect) in our current system of banker-generated and federally-regulated slavery.

Bills, or potential future laws, are either introduced in the U.S. House of Representatives (the people's House) or in the Senate (until the fraudulent passage of the 17th Amendment, the States' representation in the federal legislative process). Once a bill is introduced and passed in either of these bodies, it is then sent to the other one. Once is it passed by BOTH bodies, each version is compared to see if it was passed in identical form. If there are any differences, as there often are, it is sent to a "conference committee" where both sides discuss and agree to compromise on a piece of legislation that is acceptable to both bodies. Once that is accomplished, the now mutually agreed upon piece of legislation is sent to whichever puppet is the acting head holding the title of "President of the United States." After he signs said legislation, it is then sent to the proper administrative or regulatory agency that is responsible for administering laws of that subject matter or in those specific areas. These agencies are often referred to as the "alphabet soup agencies," because they normally utilize abbreviations to identify themselves. We are all familiar with them, i.e., IRS, BATF, EPA, OSHA, ad nausea.

These agencies now have a bona fide law, passed by both houses of Congress and signed by the President, which provides them with jurisdiction and control, as set forth in the Bill enacted into law. However, the job of the administrative agency is to turn this "big law," if you will, into what are referred to as "little laws." Congress does NOT pass these "little laws," although Congress does have the power to alter or abolish them. Of course, they seldom, if ever, do. Are you surprised? These "little laws" are often referred to as "policy." This is the way that a "regulated class" is governed and controlled. These "little laws" are officially called "regulations" and must be properly promulgated, or 'passed' by the governing administrative or regulatory agency using the procedures set forth in the APA. This is the area where the 'original intent' of Congress is altered, shifted and changed to suit someone's agenda. One of the ways that regulations can be challenged, when someone believes that the agency has gone astray, is by filing lawsuits that contest "the original intent of the Congress" in passing the original legislation. You may have heard that phrase, "original intent of Congress" referred to in the past.

There are three different and distinct types of regulations and each has different purposes. They also affect different groups of regulated entities. I will not go into all of them in any depth, as they do not apply to everyone. The regulations that do apply to everyone have what is termed "general applicability," and we will cover them in some detail.

The first two types of regulations are called either "statements of policy" or "interpretative" regulations. They are exactly what they are named: "statements of policy" are simply that, statements placed in the legal organ of the country, the Federal Register. "Interpretative" regulations apply to people within that agency or, I believe, the federal government in general. Please bear in mind that I did this research over 15 years ago and am, with this relatively trivial point, relying totally on memory.

The Federal Register can be found in any law library or on-line. The reason they have to be published in the 'legal organ' of the country is found in a little two-word phrase that everyone should have heard at least 50 times in their lifetime and comes right out of the Fifth Amendment to the U.S. Constitution. That phrase is "Due Process." Due Process is extremely important to understand. That little two-word phrase is the underpinning of our legal system. Simply put, Due Process is defined as every person's constitutionally-protected right to "notice and the right to be heard."

The third type of regulation is a totally different animal, however. It is termed a **"substantive"** regulation. This third type of regulation that is promulgated by 'all' Administrative or Regulatory Agencies has total and complete "general applicability." That means that is a binding regulation, "little law," on everyone that is in the regulated group and gives that particular agency vast "enforcement power." Because of their "general applicability," these types of regulations MUST be promulgated in a 'very' specific order, way and manner. This procedure, spelled out in the Administrative Procedures Act, is written in the U.S. Code by Congress to govern the actions and procedures of these agencies. The APA is published in Title 5, United States Code, section 552, *et seq*. Again, all of this information is coming totally from memory. I take the time with this because it is important that you understand the regulatory system and the manner and prescription by which it operates. The procedure that MUST be followed by every Administrative or Regulatory Agency in promulgating a regulation with "general applicability" is called **"Notice & Comment."**

Any regulation that has the general force and effect of law over the regulated group by the promulgating agency has to go through an extremely specific procedure. Once again, this procedure is spelled out very clearly in the Administrative Procedures Act. The initial step in the procedure is called **"Notice of Proposed Rulemaking."** If you look through the Federal Register, you will see different regulations from different agencies with this bold heading. The reason that this is required is, again, to adhere to the very foundation of our legal system - "Due Process," "notice and the right to be heard."

The first step required by the agency is to publish the proposed regulation and notify people that a regulation, possibly affecting them is being proposed. This is the "notice," or first step, of Due Process. The regulation will then be posted under that specific heading. It will state all the pertinent information that the agency is initially proposing. Because they must adhere to the Administrative Procedures Act, the agency will ALWAYS, NO EXCEPTION, place a statement at the end of the proposed regulation. The statement says that if you have any "comment," you can write 'so and so' at the address listed before some 'effective date,' usually 60-90 days in the future. It will also state the exact address to where the comment is to be sent and to whom. Anyone who thinks that the regulation has elements contained within it that they do not agree with, can register a "comment" with the person named. If you wish to file a "comment" concerning the proposed regulation, you are invited to send your 'comment' on whatever aspect of the proposed regulation you are particularly interested in.

Obviously, this is usually some type of objection. The mandated procedure at that point is for the Administrative or Regulatory Agency to take all the comments submitted in the comment period, reviews them and evaluates them in respect to the proposed substantive regulation. After review and evaluation, the proposed regulation is then reissued in the Federal Register under the heading **"Notice of Final Rulemaking."** That final form of the regulation does not take effect for a period of time in the future, which will be clearly stated, usually from 60-90 days. It is ONLY THEN that this "substantive" regulation, one with "general applicability," can take effect on the regulated group, at which point the Administrative Agency is given legal enforcement power. This second step, the "comment" step, fulfills the second half of our important phrase Due Process. It is the right-to-be-heard part of that important phrase and was obviously designed by Congress to comply with the Due Process Clause of the Fifth Amendment.

If this new regulation is an updated version of a previously promulgated regulation there will be notification (in brackets) at the end of that regulation (substantive or otherwise) as to exactly what issue of the Federal Register it was last published and on which page number it can be found. You are able, if needed, to go back and trace the entire history of any regulation that is promulgated by any agency to see exactly how it was published and promulgated. By knowing and understanding the three different types of regulations, to whom they apply and the exact process which must be adhered to by whichever agency you are researching, you can easily find out which type of regulation it is. In understanding this process, it is easy to see if the regulation you are researching has "general applicability" or not. If it is a regulation that applies to you, a once-private, now-federal citizen, it MUST have gone through the strict **"Notice & Comment"** procedure!

I can tell you personally the way I came to learn and understand this process. Like many of you may now be doing, I was fighting my greatest opponent, the IRS, during the 1990s. The reason I took so much time and exerted so much effort to understand this was that I was contesting an IRS summons for books and records that had been sent to the bank I was using at the time. I filed suit in U.S. District Court in the Northern District of Georgia against the summons. As I was writing briefs and studying in an attempt to win my battle, I started being taught by one of my teachers about regulations. What I found (unfortunately after the initial hearing was completed) was that the regulation the IRS was using could be traced back to the original IRS regulations promulgated in 1954!

After I had traced that particular regulation back to its origin, I discovered that the original regulation was promulgated as an "interpretative" regulation! Due to the fact that it was NOT promulgated under the required "Notice & Comment" method REQUIRED for general applicability by the APA, that regulation ONLY had any force and effect over government employees and not the public at large! So very many people have lost so very much due to the IRS utilizing a regulation that was NEVER properly promulgated for 'general applicability' and DOES NOT EFFECT THEM? Unless the above information is understood and applied, anyone receiving a "summons for books and records" will simply comply under the implied threat of the dreaded and feared IRS. This is one method that can be utilized to fight the federal government from within the system administratively. BUT, these points MUST be brought up in any court battle at the District Court level. If not raised and contested at that level, those issues cannot be brought up later in the process if one might choose to appeal the lower level decision.

In reality, the first place to fight any agency action is by contesting it within the particular administrative agency that has initiated the action against you. It is a fundamental rule of the courts that you must "exhaust your administrative remedies" before filing any suit in U.S. District Court.

Now, armed with this background and understanding, you may ask why am I devoting so much effort to teach you about administrative agencies, why are they so important? It is the logical fact that any agency can ONLY promulgate regulations and enforce them on the group that they "regulate!" Now comes the $64,000 question! Who, exactly, ARE these "regulated groups" and, even more importantly, how does one become a member of such groups or what makes one a "regulated entity?"

Administrative or Regulatory Agencies maintain an exhaustive listing of their "little laws." These are the completed and standing regulations that govern their responsibility, conduct and procedures and 'exactly who and how' they are by law allowed to regulate. These sets of pamphlet-type books are found in any law library and appear in a set of books called the "Code of Federal Regulations" or, "C.F.R." There are 50 Titles of C.F.R.'s, which correspond to the 50 Titles of the United Stated Code. These titles govern the subject matter areas of responsibility of the corresponding agency. In the opening book of whichever title of C.F.R. you are researching, there will be a statement somewhere, usually early in that title, as to EXACLTY WHO they can "regulate." In every single title, EXCEPT Title 26 C.F.R., the regulated group is comprised of "residents." In 26 C.F.R., the IRS set of regulations, at 1.1-1(a), it states plainly and clearly the three different classes of persons to whom the ENTIRE tax code of regulations apply. Those are "a citizen or resident of the United States" and, "to the extent provided in section 871(b) or 877(b), to a "non-resident alien individual." In section 1.1-1(c) of 26 C.F.R, on the next page, of course, it goes on to identify exactly WHO IS a "citizen." "Every person born or naturalized in the United States and SUBJECT TO ITS JURISDICTION IS A CITIZEN." This is, almost word for word, a repeat of the first sentence of the 14th Amendment to the Constitution!

The reason this section is so terribly important to our understanding of 'exactly' what has been done to us is simply this. We have already seen in the application for a U.S. Passport that there are two separate and distinct, "mutually exclusive," if you will, types of legal statuses of "persons." Likewise, the IRS regulations tell us 'exactly' to which persons the income tax code applies and against whom they may be enforced. We see quite plainly that there are three different and distinct classes of persons to whom the Tax Code applies. If one goes back to the listed exception sections of 26 C.F.R. at section 1.1- 1(a), you will see that the two exception sections are 871(b) and 877(b). Should one take the time, energy and effort to research these two exceptions, you will find that the taxes imposed under these two sections correspond precisely to the types of taxes imposed under the original Constitution of the United States of America on a free Citizen of the United States. Those methods of taxation prescribed in the Constitution are termed "excise" and "capitation." These two methods of constitutionally prescribed taxation must be "uniform" and "apportioned." The capitation method was one of the original reasons for the census being required, because the population within a state dictated the amount of tax that would be assessed to each person if there was legislation passed for such a capitation or "head" tax.

So, there you have it! Two types of legal statuses, mutually exclusive, listed in the passport application and three types of legal statuses, also mutually exclusive, listed in the taxing regulations. Nonresident aliens would not apply for a U.S. passport, so their status is not represented in the passport application. AGAIN, BOTH documents list mutually exclusive legal statuses.

Both the passport application and Treasury Regulation §1.1-1(a) refer to citizens of the United States. We know that the citizenship referred to in both places is the citizenship conferred by the 14th Amendment upon the four million African-Americans freed as a result of the Civil War or War Between the States, as it is also called. As we shall see below, the citizenship conferred meant that the citizen owed to the United States *"direct and immediate allegiance." Elk v. Wilkins*, 112 U.S. 94, 102 (1884).

The type of 'allegiance' owed was that required of serfs in England. See *United States v. Wong Kim Ark*, 169 U.S.649, 707 (1898) (Fuller, J., dissenting) (describing the citizenship rule adopted by the majority as "the outcome of the connection in feudalism between the individual and the soil on which he lived, and the allegiance due was that of liege men to their liege lord"). I cannot bring myself to believe that free men and women of three fourths of the States would knowingly have passed a constitutional amendment with the intention to consign themselves, their children and their posterity into voluntary servitude, the English, French and common-law kind of slavery practiced in much of the world for untold centuries. I will discuss this more completely below.

The Treasury Regulation at § 1.1-1(a) lists three classes of persons: citizens of the United States, residents (meaning resident aliens), and nonresident aliens. If, as we shall see, we are not the citizen-serfs referred to in the 14th Amendment and if we are not resident aliens, as defined in the Internal Revenue Code ("IRC") itself, we must, by mere process of elimination, be "nonresident aliens," as defined in the IRC at § 7701(b)(1)(B).[1]

The passport application mentions only two different classes of persons: citizens of the United States and U.S. nationals. Again, if we are not the U.S. citizen-serfs referred to in the application, we must, again, by process of elimination, be U.S. Nationals.

Once more, by logical deduction, it appears that free Americans must fall within the class of persons called "nonresident aliens" in the IRC and as "U.S. nationals" in the passport application.

If, then, free Americans are both nonresident aliens and U.S. nationals, one might be tempted to ask: nonresident and alien to what?

Before we can answer this question we must recognize that it contains two words that are equivocal in nature and we must recognize their intended meaning. Those words are, of course, *resident* and *alien*. Before attempting to answer the question we must have a clear understanding of the nature of the residency ascribed to that so-called *resident*, and we must understand the nature of the citizenship ascribed to the so-called *citizen*.

The 14th Amendment established a new class of citizenship and residency that did not previously exist. It introduced the term *subject* into the constitution, and that term cannot be understood without reference to its antonym, s*overeign*. The subject owes allegiance to the sovereign. Without a *sovereign* to whom the *subject* owes allegiance, there is no subjection and there can be no subjects. Who is the sovereign in this case? Is it the central government in Washington, D.C.? Is it the individual or collective States of the Union, or is it the people who formed the states and, through them, formed the Union? When the question is posed in this manner, its answer is obvious and discussed in more detail below.

What is the nature of the residency of the 14th Amendment? Briefly, that class of residency is the residency that was created by the 14th Amendment along with its *subjects*. We can speculate about its characteristics but it is unnecessary to do so. All we need to know is that it is permanently connected to the *subject* and if one is not a *subject,* resident to the newly-created residency of the 14th Amendment, one is not a *resident,* at least not within the meaning and intent of that Amendment.

So, armed with this understanding we can proceed to answer the question previously posed: nonresident and alien to exactly what?

Answer: nonresident to the state residency defined in the 14th Amendment (recall that this amendment made the Freedmen both national citizen-serfs and state residents, "completely subject to the political jurisdiction of the United States and owing them direct and immediate allegiance"), and alien to the serf-citizenship conferred by the 14th Amendment.

Recall, also, that the passport application did state that "our laws on citizenship are very complex." Are you beginning to appreciate how much of an understatement that comment was?

Why, then, are free Americans also U.S. nationals in the passport process?

Consider this: in England, there are only two classes of persons – subjects and a sovereign; England has no *citizens*, as we use that term in the United States. Now, Queen Elizabeth is certainly not a subject; she is the sovereign. Is she also a 'national' of the nation of England?

At dictionary.com, we find the definition of 'national,' when used as a noun: "*a citizen or subject of a particular nation who is entitled to its protection.*" Do you think that the Queen is entitled to the protection of England? The answer is obvious. Do you think she is a subject of England? Hardly! Quite obviously, she is entitled to England's protection, she is not a subject, and, because

England has no *citizens*, as we use that term, she must be the sovereign-national of England.

Just as the Queen is the sovereign-national of England, so also, free Americans are the sovereign-nationals of the United States. See *Chisholm v. Georgia*, 2 U.S. 419, 471-72 (1793) ("at the Revolution, the sovereignty devolved on the people; and they are truly the sovereigns of the country, but they are sovereigns without subjects (unless the African slaves among us may be so called) and have none to govern but themselves; the citizens of America are equal as fellow citizens, and as joint tenants in the sovereignty").

Who among us would ever have believed that our government officials would refer to free Americans as "nonresident aliens" in the Internal Revenue Code and as "nationals" in the passport application? Can you see the treachery and deception of words employed by these officials? Can you see why I have felt compelled to spread this knowledge as far and as wide as possible? You, my dear Reader, are the means of spreading this knowledge.

As you read, study and think about the information presented and documented in the remainder of this small but powerful book, you should easily come to understand the deceitful trick that has been played on the populace of America, our great and beloved country! Even more important, this gives you an insight into how our enemy controls the entire populace throughout all aspects of their web of lies and deceit.

Read on! You should now have the necessary background to see the following subject matter and points made in a much clearer and more easily understandable framework.

Part II

"The moral of the story is that words are mankind's greatest weapon; as shown in this quote," 'There are weapons that are simply thoughts, attitudes, prejudices to be found only in the minds of men.'" - Rod Serling, *The Monsters Are Due on Maple Street*, S01E22 of *the TWILIGHT ZONE*

I begin the second part of this book with two statements for the record, from the record. I would like you to read these now. We will cover them again toward the end of this book.

I present two solid statements, from the Congressional Record, of 'exactly' what has happened to our people. These two statements are by loyal American politicians probably more accurately referred to as "statesmen." I know there are many more, but the statements by these two men are extremely illustrative, quite concise and descriptive. Of the two, the most recent one is by former Ohio Congressman James Traficant, who was recently released after seven years behind bars as a political prisoner. The second is from former, long-time Pennsylvania Congressman Louis T. McFadden who was Chairman of the House Banking Committee for approximately 20 years. In studying McFadden, and after reading a number of his statements on the House floor, I was amazed to read that the last time he ran for the House he was nominated by all three major parties at the time, the Republicans, the Democrats and the Populist Party. I know of no other American statesman who has had this much of a total wide acceptance by the populace, let alone the feuding political parties!

Congressional Record, March 17, 1993, Vol. 33, page H-1303. The speaker is **Rep. James Traficant** (Ohio) (obviously done in Special Orders where no one is present):

> *"Prior to 1913, most Americans owned clear, allodial title to property, free and clear of any liens of mortgages until the Federal Reserve Act (1913) "Hypothecated" all property within the Federal United States to the Board of Governors of the Federal Reserve, in which the Trustees (stockholders) held legal title. The U.S. Citizen (tenant, franchisee) was registered as a "beneficiary" of the trust via his/her birth certificate. In 1933, the Federal United*

States hypothecated all of the present and future properties, assets, and labor of their "subjects," the 14th Amendment U.S. Citizen to the Federal Reserve System. In return, the Federal Reserve System agreed to extend the federal United States Corporation all of the credit "money substitute" it needed.

Like any debtor, the Federal United States government had to assign collateral and security to their creditors as a condition of the loan. Since the Federal United States didn't have any assets, they assigned the private property of their "economic slaves," the U.S. Citizens, as collateral against the federal debt. They also pledged the unincorporated federal territories, national parks, forests, birth certificates, and nonprofit organizations as collateral against the federal debt. All has already been transferred as payment to the international bankers.

Unwittingly, America has returned to its pre-American Revolution feudal roots whereby all land is held by a sovereign and the common people had no rights to hold allodial title to property. Once again, We the People are the tenants and sharecroppers renting our own property from a Sovereign in the guise of the Federal Reserve Bank. We the People have exchanged one master for another."

NOTE: This passage, attributed to Congressman Jim Trafficant, was written in during the initial writing of this book in 2005. I have been informed by patriot attorney Larry Becraft that this is 'patriot mythology.' Having long ago moved from all of the research notes and resources from those days I cannot say where I acquired the information. However, I think the passage should be left intact and in the book. The first reason for doing so is whoever did write this had such a total and accurate command of what has happened. The second reason is that, if Jim Trafficant didn't say it, he should have! This certainly would have been an historically accurate picture of the events of last century and what has happened to America. (*RSS*)

Our second example is from Congressman Louis T. McFadden in Congress; from the Congressional Record, Friday, June 8th, 1934.

> *"Frankfurter has been furnishing most of the legal brains for the outfit, and it is said that no legal position of any consequence can be secured by any lawyer in the present administration without it has first had the approval of Frankfurter. And it is a startling fact, in connection with this, that most of the legal advisers, especially in key positions, are Jews. Felix Frankfurter's adept student and protégé, Jerome N. Frank, general counsel of the Agricultural Adjustment Administration, delivered an address before the Association of American Law Schools, thirty-first annual meeting, at Chicago, December 30, 1933, on Experimental Jurisprudence and the New Deal.*
>
> *A reading of this address shows the contempt of the Frankfurter lawyers for the Constitution of the land and an expressed determination to obviate and avoid constitutional barriers in their administration of the Nation's affairs. Those in charge of the plan and its administration in the United States have for years considered methods for accomplishing their ends without regard to the Constitution of the United States. They recognize the fact that the National Industrial Recovery Act did not give them all of the power they desired in order to break down the barriers enacted in our Constitution, preserving certain rights to the various States of the Union, as well as other features.*

> *Therefore, in the promulgation of the various codes affecting industry and agriculture throughout the country, they have sought to compel, browbeat, and bulldoze the business interests of this country to engage in private contract so that they would have the power to require the business interests of the Nation to do their wishes regardless of the Constitution.*
>
> *The "new-deal" lawyers now have no hesitancy in appearing in court and asserting that* ***private citizens can contract away their constitutional rights***. *It has been through this method that they have broken down State lines and invaded the most private affairs of our citizens. It will be through this method, for instance, that the little retailer of the country will be driven out of business and chain-store-system control by them put into operation, just as they are attempting in England."*

In his class, John taught us that the desire for 'freedom' is perhaps the most powerful impulse of the human heart. He related a story written by the radio personality Paul Harvey in a Los Angeles newspaper, January 1, 1980. Here are Mr. Harvey's own words from that article:

> **CHIMPANZEE VOICES PLEA:** *I've just endured one of the most cold- sweat experiences of my life. I heard the "voice of an animal".*
>
> *When I relate my experience of having heard an animal "talk", I am not referring to the mimicry of a parrot. Here's what happened. My son, Paul, researching a "Rest of the Story" story for broadcast, became acquainted with a research*

project at the University of Oklahoma. There they have been teaching an animal to talk--- specifically a 15 year old female chimpanzee named Washoe. This is the basic recognition communication, mostly single unit: big, small, up, down. Since 1966 this chimpanzee has learned 140 signs in Standard American Sign Language. After all this learning and more learning, the project directors decided that Washoe was prepared now to "conceptualize." In lay language, instead of imitating some human's words—the chimp was ready to express thoughts of her own. She had learned enough words to cross-reference those words and "originate" expressions of her own. Now, understand Washoe is a pampered animal in the University Laboratory – well fed, physically comfortable, safe from harm. She had "security". And yet—when she was able to put words together on her own into a phrase—these were the first three. And she has said them again – repeatedly. To visitors the voice from the cage is saying: "LET ME OUT!"

Washoe's cry for FREEDOM says it all. No one wants to live in a cage. No matter how well fed, how pampered you may be, no matter how secure you may feel, the cry for FREEDOM, "Let me out," is perhaps stronger even than the desire to live. That is why soldiers will throw themselves on live grenades in a foxhole, to preserve the lives of their fellow soldiers. We will, under certain circumstances, give our last full measure, even our very lives, for the sake of preserving freedom for ourselves and our loved ones. That is the reason I left the land of my birth and moved to Argentina – like Washoe, I wanted to be FREE! That is the reason I have devoted my life to spreading the knowledge I have acquired – I know others also want to be free!

At the beginning, let me state that I was exposed to these concepts very early in my awakening. In fact, I learned of these concepts within the first 30 days of what has become the meat of my life's work. Because of that fact, I've been able to look at everything in the world, for over 18 years at this point, through what I call *They Live* glasses. And after writing that sentence, a week later, Jeff Rense put a Bush "they live" jpeg as his graphic on www.rense.com.

I was born at the front end of the notorious 'baby boomer' generation. Being in college in the turbulent 60s I, like many reading this book, knew in my 'heart of hearts' that something wasn't 'right' with the country and the world. I venture to say that my awareness started with the assassination of John F. Kennedy. Being pretty young at that time and being like most young people at that age, I was totally naïve. That murder, the Viet Nam war escalating, Robert Kennedy, Martin Luther King, Kent State, Democratic National Convention, etc. I just KNEW that something was wrong but kept accessing the establishment media for my reality. I remember having verbally abusive arguments with my Father at the dinner table over Richard Nixon and the entire Watergate Scandal.

Years later, my favorite brother-in-law would tell me about the secret groups that would meet, plan and scheme to control the world and that their meetings would NEVER be covered or even so much as mentioned in the media. I remember it distinctly as the first time I had ever heard of the CFR & Trilateral Commission. He didn't know much more (he had probably been approached by a member of the John Birch Society, I've always thought) and I was intrigued but had no track to run on, so the info was filed away in the 'intrigued' part of the back of my mind.

A few years into the 80s, I was coming out of some meeting of some sort and someone gave me a red covered book. I glanced at it, kept it and when I got home, immediately put it up on the shelf where it stayed for another 8-10 years. That book was *To Harass Our People*, by Congressman Hansen. If you don't know who Hansen is you should familiarize yourself with his story.

Those were the seeds that lay long dormant, until July of 1992.

I found the tax movement in 1992 or, perhaps more accurately stated, the tax movement found me! The first time I saw any information on it was a video-taped presentation by a gentleman named Al Carter. That was on Thursday July 16, 1992. The reason I remember so accurately is that this was the night that Bill Clinton accepted the Democratic nomination for the first time in Madison Square Garden. I wanted to see his speech, so I stopped the video to watch it. My intention was to continue watching the video a short time later when Clinton was finished speaking. You may or may not remember that was the longest acceptance speech ever delivered in the history of American politics. It lasted around 2 hours. I had to work the next day and had something planned for Friday night, so I didn't get the chance to watch the second half of the video until Saturday morning. I literally couldn't wait to get up, go downstairs and put that tape in to see what else Al Carter had to offer. I was already blown away and all of Carter's 'proofs' were still in the back half of that video.

That Saturday morning, after watching the video I picked my jaw up off the ground and asked myself the same question I'm sure many of you have asked yourselves, "if they can screw us this bad without anyone really knowing about it, what the hell else are they doing to us?"

Not having any information other than the public library in

Marietta, Georgia, that's where I started, in the reference section. The first document I found is attached. Here is the "pertinent part" I found that told me immediately that we had a gigantic problem. I had NO IDEA at the time just what a nightmare I had awakened to find.

The entire document will be at the end of this book, if you care to read it in its entirety. This is, I now know, the total blueprint of how they have taken over nations and is a blueprint they still seem to follow very closely, if not precisely.

> *"The conditions of the loan seem to us to touch very nearly the administrative independence of China itself; and this administration does not feel that it ought, even by implication, to be a party to those conditions. The responsibility on its part which would be implied in requesting the bankers to undertake* **the loan might conceivably go to the length, in some unhappy contingency, of forcible interference in the financial, and even the political, affairs of that great Oriental state**, *just now awakening to a consciousness of its power and of its obligations to its people.*
>
> *The conditions include not only the pledging of particular taxes, <u>some of them antiquated and burdensome</u>, to secure the loan but also* **the administration of those taxes by foreign agents**. *The responsibility on the part of our government implied in the encouragement of a loan thus secured and administered is plain enough and is obnoxious to the principles upon which the government of our people rests."* - **Woodrow Wilson**: *Repudiation of "Dollar Diplomacy," American Journal of International Law*, Vol. VII, pp. 338-399

I think that even a person newly exposed to all of this traitorous activity can spot a correlation to modern days. If this isn't a "blueprint," I don't know what is! By the way, if you have ever heard that the IRS is 'not' a federal government agency, this statement should give you some insight into their general plan.

Two days later, someone called and told me there was tax meeting in town on the following Tuesday. You couldn't have held me back with a team of wild horses. I have ALWAYS been a "truth-seeker" and I had finally found a thread to follow and a gigantic track to run on!

Tuesday came and I was at the hotel early to get a good seat. That was my first and only time to see Phil Marsh in person. His info contained many errors (that's why they let Marsh go for 5 years and also exactly why they let many people with misinformation keep going even today). I watched the presentation and after was able to purchase some books, so now I really had the track to start running. Every time I saw an address that offered additional information, I would send a letter, asking for a complete list of books, publications, etc. This was several years before the Internet was providing access and research for this type of information. At that time, it was much harder to find sources of information of the type I was now seeking than it is now.

Several weeks later I get another phone call from my Russian friend. He said, "there's another tax meeting in town tonight." "Where?" I asked. He said, "It's a guy named Benson, that's all I know." Having already learned about Bill Benson and his proof of the non-passage of the 16th Amendment, I was thrilled to have the opportunity to see him talk and hear his story! It wasn't Bill Benson nor was it Wayne Bentson. The speaker was a very unpretentious, portly fellow named John Benson and an authoritative guy named Glenn Ambort. They proceeded to absolutely blow a young neophyte's mind. If you've never been exposed to very complicated legal concepts when you have literally no background or solid familiarity, you don't know what it's like, but you probably will, as you read a little further. They were trying to explain and teach us stuff that, initially, was miles over our heads. I was totally blown away, but, even though I really did not understand all the information, I knew the info was important. I could just sense in my gut that there was something of great importance in what they were telling us about. I was more than intrigued and stuck with it.

It wasn't but about 6 months later before a 27-man armed IRS/BATF SWAT team raided John's & Glenn's home and office in Las Vegas and their offices in four other locations. They arrested no one but did hold them at gunpoint for 8 hours in order to take all their computers, files & work product. They had been teaching for a mere six months at the time of the raid. We knew, from that moment that John & Glenn were onto something that the Treasury/IRS was freaked out about. The raid fit the old cliché *"if you are catching flack, you know you are over the target."* The reason for that has become very clear to me since that time and especially in the last few years.

Later, John attempted to enter the political arena in Utah; he ran for the Democratic nomination for U.S. Senator, hoping to run against Orin Hatch in the November election of 1994. Glenn ran his campaign. Evidently, it didn't take much of that activity before the feds decided to prosecute these two and thereby keep their message out of the public eye. It took over six years and much court activity - appeals, motions, appeal of motions, etc. – but they finally convicted these two dangerous political criminals attempting to clarify the "complicated citizenship laws" and put them away in federal prison – 5 ½ years for John, 8 ½ for Glenn – on trumped up "conspiracy" charges. I doubt that you would be surprised if I told you that they were 'convicted' on perjured testimony. I promise you the only conspiracy going on was at the federal level from the federal prosecutor and the Judge! However, I have come to realize EXACTLY WHY these two WERE so dangerous! Someone had finally figured out the key to not only the taxation system but to the **_ENTIRE_** federal system that has enslaved the American people and taken over the country.

What I started learning for the first time was how our government was designed to work and how it has been changed. I started reading voraciously in the subjects of law, history, etc. One of my very dear friends in Atlanta calls it being "horizontally strung out." I'm sure some of you will relate to this sequence. You get into one main body of study, Law, for example. You study Law, a lifetime body of study by itself, when you find out that the monetary system isn't what it seems to be, so you drop your Law study and start studying Economics and Monetary Theory. You get into that deep and complicated subject and you find out there's a connection to something that is wrong with the medical system, so you stop studying Economics and start studying the medical system. In your medical study, another lifetime study, you find out the medical industry is being dominated by government, so you stop studying medicine and switch to government and civics. Then you have Chem-trails, Morgellon's Disease, RFID Chips, privacy concerns, etc.

Any of these topics is itself practically a lifetime study, but they all tie in together. To have a good understanding, you have to have some working knowledge of how they interact individually and collectively. Hence, the term: horizontally strung-out!

Early in my studies, I came across references to the Chinese General and author, Sun Tzu, and his timeless book *The Art of War*. Coming from a military family I was intrigued as I had never heard of Sun Tzu. What I learned was that virtually every conqueror in history knew about and followed Sun Tzu's teachings. Sun Tzu said many things however, for our discussion here, just know that Sun Tzu advocates a total campaign of deception. If your enemy thinks you're here, be over there. Where he thinks you're strong, be weak. Whatever you can do to make your enemy think the exact opposite is the winning tactic. In fact, the ultimate goal of Sun Tzu's teachings is that you can win not only a battle but also an entire war without firing a single shot. However, one thing he stated hit me hard because it made such total and complete sense. Sun Tzu was very adamant; he stated, **"If you don't know your enemy and you don't know yourself, you have no chance of winning ANY battle."**

> *"If you know the enemy and know yourself, you need not fear the result of a hundred battles. If you know yourself but not the enemy, for every victory gained you will also suffer a defeat. If you know neither the enemy nor yourself, you will succumb in every battle."* - **Sun Tzu**

I totally understood this statement; it made complete logical sense. I had already discovered, even at this early stage, that all of the previous ideas I had held concerning the federal government were already shot full of holes. From that point on, everything I read and learned got filtered through my Sun Tzu glasses. That type of approach certainly puts things into a much clearer perspective.

As a very specific and exact example of Sun Tzu, do you know that the slogan of Mossad is, *"By way of deception, we shall make* war'"? That motto is classic Sun Tzu and, believe me, every intelligence service in the world utilizes these very same techniques. I shouldn't have to tell you, at this stage that they are very accomplished at their craft; just look at history through your Sun Tzu and *They Live* glasses!

It seemed that the more time I put into study, the more questions arose! I imagine every one of you reading this, if you start thinking about it, can see the Sun Tzu influence all around you in current and past events, not only in our country, but the entire world.

I have a media background. During my many years in radio and the music industry, one question that particularly interested me came in an unsolicited letter in my mailbox: *"Does SONY stand for Standard Oil of New York?"* That one particular question really stuck a chord with me! I was teaching several media courses at a local trade school in Atlanta at the time. One of my bosses' wives was the highest-ranking woman in the world for the Bank of Japan, which had a branch in Atlanta. I asked him the question, and he too was intrigued, as he has previously owned a recording studio. He went home and asked his wife to ask around the office. A short time later, when we were both in the school admin office, I asked him, *"Did Linda find out anything about the name SONY?"* He said that she had asked two people at work. The first one said, *"I don't know, but it is really amazing how such a small company could become so big and powerful after the war."* The second person said, *"In the Japanese language, all words come from the culture and society. He called it 'kanji' and SONY has NO KANJI in Japanese."* At that point, the only higher up to ask was the bank branch president - her immediate boss; she just flat refused to ask him. Even she got the idea pretty quickly, it appeared! I've since come to be 100% positive that the answer to the question is an emphatic YES! It's owned and controlled, along with Japan, by the

Rockefeller Empire. This must have been the deal after WWII: Rothschilds take Europe; Rockefeller's get the Orient countries. Not to mention that, also a number of years ago, when Rockefeller Plaza was sold, it was purchased by SONY. What an amazing coincidence!

At that point, I started thinking more in the terms of being VERY specific about the words that I used. Here's a trap that virtually everyone has fallen into. We all literally call those who administer our country "the government." That is NOT ACCURATE! **WE ARE THE GOVERNMENT! They are the "AGENTS" of government!** We 'elect' representatives (agents to us), and they go to DC to legislate ON OUR BEHALF. They appoint 'agents' to administrate those laws. We ARE the government; they are AGENTS OF GOVERNMENT!

Once you start identifying them as "the government," they are then a non-descript blob, no face and no name. They are actually "agents." As such, by operation of law, they have specific duties and responsibilities. If they do not execute those duties correctly or they are over-zealous in such execution, they then are "personally" liable OUTSIDE of their government positions, duties and responsibilities. Those rogue agents can be prosecuted in their 'personal capacity' for acting outside of those areas of responsibilities! Not identifying them correctly puts a mental block in our minds that they are larger than life and untouchable. This is simply not true! However, it is the impression they want to convey and have largely succeeded in establishing in our minds.

I learned that there are TWO types of lies: **Lies of *commission*** and **lies of *omission***. Lies of commission are outright lies with which we are all familiar. Lies of omission are an entirely different animal. These are the pertinent parts or facts of a story that are intentionally left out or not included. Both of these types of lies are used on us daily!

Another very important thing I learned early on was that we are always shown the second hit or blow! Just like a player fight at a sporting event, many times the referee only seems to see the second blow and penalizes the wrong player. So, when we see things, such as the recent incursion into Lebanon, Iraq or Afghanistan, I know automatically that whoever is being blamed is the innocent party.

~ WORDS MEAN THINGS ~
What I quickly came to realize is this: as a general rule, "WHATEVER it is that they are directing your attention toward, if you want to find the real truth (figuratively or literally), **first**, look 180 degrees in the opposite direction! I cannot stress how important an idea and point this is! The actual truth, regardless what they may claim, always seems to be in the opposite direction. To understand our oppressors and traditional enemies, you have to understand not only how they think, but also how they employ their tactics to suit their dastardly purposes. This "opposite direction" method is the first and surest method of unraveling whatever pile of garbage they are attempting to sell you. They have used it over and over and over again. Why do they continue to use it? Simply because it works! The dumbed down sheeple buy it every single time! More classic Sun Tzu tactics!

Do you know that, in a lawsuit, attorneys can define a word in any manner they choose *IF* they are representing the plaintiffs? All they have to do is spell out that redefined word or phrase in the suit and identify the word or terms. Throughout the rest of the suit, those specific words retain those definitions. Black can be redefined as white or up as down and, for the remainder of whatever is under consideration, the new meaning is whatever they have stated it is. Pretty nifty little trick, huh?

Let's examine some specifics from one of our favorite nursery stories, *Alice in Wonderland*. Have any of you ever heard that *Alice in Wonderland* is a political document? It definitely is! In fact, several of the most popular children's stories of all time have heavy political overtones. Not only *Alice in Wonderland*, which we will examine in more detail momentarily, but also the *Wizard of Oz* and *Little Orphan Annie*. In 'Annie,' one of the main characters, Big Daddy "Warbucks," is actually supposed to be Paul Warburg, "Big Daddy Warburg!"

Warburg is one of the main men who were able to deceive the American public and Congress into passing the Federal Reserve Act in 1913. This is the legislation that has led to today's present disastrous worldwide financial situation. Our current 'masters' love to boast that "we tell them what we're doing to them but they are so stupid they don't understand; therefore, they need us to control them." I think their psychiatrists would call that a supreme rationalization to suppress guilt. They are satanic Psychopaths, plain and simple.

While studying to be a paralegal at an accredited institute, I found this direct quote in the very first page of a legal research book published by NOLO Press.

> "**When I use a word**," Humpty Dumpty said, in a rather scornful tone, "**it means just what I choose it to mean – no more no less**." "**The question is**," said Alice, "**whether you can make words mean so many different things?**" "**The question is**," said Humpty Dumpty, "**which is to be master – that's all**." Alice In Wonderland, Lewis Carroll. (Emphasis added)

"*Words mean what I say they mean Alice*," said the Mad Hatter.

On the topic of Alice, have you ever heard the story of why hat makers were called "Mad Hatters?" At that time in England, sons generally followed their fathers in their professions. Making hats required hand-pushing needles through the heavy felt material of which hats were made. The hats were then steamed to make them pliable for shaping. They would use steam to help form the heavy material evidently processed with some type of mercury. The hatters would then inhale the fumes released from the steaming process. The material used was thick and dense. Because of this difficulty, 'Hatters' would dip their needles in mercury to help ease the passage of the needle through the heavy material. Of course, it seems certain that many would not wear a thimble and prick their fingers. The pure mercury would enter the bloodstream or be inhaled in the steam, and they would eventually "go mad" from the poisonous effects of the mercury. <u>Can you possibly conceive that our Agents of government and their controllers DO NOT KNOW ABOUT MERCURY POISONING?</u>

Here's some information on Alice from Wikipedia:

> *The members of the boating party that first heard Carroll's tale all show up in Chapter 3 ("A Caucus-Race and a Long Tale") in one form or another. There is, of course, Alice herself, while Carroll, or Charles Dodgson, is caricatured as the Dodo. The Duck refers to Rev. Robinson Duckworth, the Lory to Lorina Liddell, and the Eaglet to Edith Liddell.*
>
> *Bill the Lizard may be a play on the name of Benjamin Disraeli. One of Tenniel's illustrations in Through the Looking Glass depicts a caricature of Disraeli, wearing a paper hat, as a passenger on a*

> train. The illustrations of the Lion and the Unicorn also bear a striking resemblance to Tenniel's Punch illustrations of Gladstone and Disraeli.
>
> The Mock Turtle speaks of a Drawling- master, "**an old conger eel**," that used to come once a week to teach "Drawling, Stretching, and Fainting in Coils." This is a reference to the art critic, **John Ruskin**, **who came once a week to the Liddell house to teach the children drawing, sketching, and painting in oils.** (The children did, in fact, learn well; Alice Liddell, for one, produced a number of skilled watercolors.)

Have you ever heard the name John Ruskin? He's got quite the place in England and in world history. He was the professor at Oxford who had a lifelong effect on a young student named Cecil Rhodes. The idea was to reassert the British Empire to the point where it would regain its past greatness when the common saying was, "the sun NEVER sets on the British Empire." Rhodes ruthlessly acquired and developed many of South Africa's gold, platinum and diamond mines. In fact, his first land purchase was from an Afrikaner family named DeBeers. In a twisted manner so typical of the super-rich, he named his first large success for the family that unknowingly sold him one of the richest diamond mines in the world. Rhodes, a homosexual, died childless, but before he died, he set up a number of trusts, six, I believe. Those trusts are still managed today by the Rothschild family. The Rothschilds managed then, as they do today, his great wealth to achieve his lifelong dream, and that of Ruskin, to see England regain mastery of the world. One has to look no further than the number of notable world 'leaders' (puppets) who have been Rhodes Scholars to connect the dots.

If you ever want to study into the origins of our situation more in depth, John Ruskin would be a very good starting point.

Part of the Wikipedia information is a picture of a really nice statue of Alice in Wonderland and cast of characters in Central Park in New York. I would be willing to bet practically everything I own that the statue was paid for and placed there by one of the Rockefeller family, Foundations or organizations. Remember how they like to tell us what they are doing to us? Now, all of you would see and understand that perfectly from seeing Alice and her cast of characters sitting on a giant mushroom in the middle of Central Park wouldn't you?

The one reason I have internalized this information so completely is that I've lived it for the last 18 years. I've made the information that we will cover in his booklet part of me, my life, how I live and how I view the world. I literally look at the world through lenses colored by the events recounted in this book. My view of world events makes perfect sense to me because I understand our common enemies and how their diabolical methods have duped our people and the people of the world. Even many of those who think they totally understand world problems do not understand these techniques and, therefore, step on verbal landmines at almost every turn. Knowing their techniques and living this information allows me, in many respects, actually to see the future. Why? Because I know my enemy, his tactics and techniques and, most importantly, really, I know his history. This has enabled me, with some certainty, to know what their next move is going to be, sometimes, as in chess, even several moves ahead. It has allowed me to position myself in front of them. This knowledge and insight has allowed me to place myself in a very desirable personal position and situation. If you've ever seen the movie *They Live* on late night TV, you know exactly what I'm talking about. See, they like to tell us what they're doing, etc., etc., etc. . . . All we have to do is learn their tactics and techniques. Then, we will be able to read the road signs. It's almost like following a map. It's like putting on the sunglasses in that movie.

Men/Women, left-brain/right-brain: women are generally much more emotionally oriented than men. This makes them much easier to manipulate by triggering emotions. A specific example of this occurred some years ago when Bill Clinton appeared in the Iowa Caucus. Immediately after his unopposed victory in 1996, Bill was crying crocodile tears when in his 'victory speech' he stated, "I've wanted to win the Iowa Caucus since I was a little boy." Research showed that the Iowa Caucus wasn't started until Clinton was in his late 20s!

I'm sure you will remember that Clinton's 'base' consisted of those 'soccer Moms.' Was he pushing their emotional buttons that day! Can't you just see all his female supporters, "he's wanted to win since he was a little boy, isn't that sweet."

On the other hand, men tend to be more analytical than emotional. It is much more difficult to utilize emotional triggers such as these to alter someone's viewpoint when they look at the world in a "2+2=4" mindset. To get the same type of effect with men, the manipulators go back and trigger false Patriotism. That's where the image of "Uncle Sam" came from during WWI. How many men have given their lives, their limbs or their health to go fight a war for patriotic ideals, when, in reality, they were fighting for the Satanist international bankers struggling for control and monopoly of the world's resources? (Read Marine Corp General Smedley Butler's *War Is A Racket*, found easily on the Internet). By pushing the patriotic or logic button to induce young men and women to volunteer for war, the manipulators are able to remove from the

Nation's gene-pool the finest young spirits this Nation has to offer. Thus, as their future agenda unfolds and becomes apparent to the masses, they will not have to face opposition from these now-departed great spirits, in many cases, the best of America.

Here's another simple example that came to me as I was watching a 2-hour documentary on Israel. There were scenes and brutal truth in that video that, believe me, our 'leaders/controllers' DO NOT want Americans to know about and work into their perspective of America's Foreign Policy. A certain Rabbi was being interviewed and was speaking about publicity and about some of the more heinous activities committed by the Israeli Defense Force. The Rabbi said, *"**All they have to hear is the word 'defense' and they quit thinking!**"* How subtle and effective their techniques are!

~ Mystery Babylon v. Babylon ~

Babylon was the first attempt to produce a New World Order. According to the Biblical account, *"a united humanity of the generations following the Great Flood, speaking a single language and migrating from the east, came to the land of Shinar, where they resolved to build a city with a tower "with its top in the heavens...lest we be scattered abroad upon the face of the Earth." God came down to see what they did and said: "They are one people and have one language, and nothing will be withholden from them which they purpose to do." So God said, "Come, let us go down and confound their speech." And so God scattered them upon the face of the Earth, and confused their languages, and they left off building the city, which was called Babel "because God there confounded the language of all the Earth."* - Genesis 11:5-8). Many people associate the confusion of the tower of Babel with Babylon.

Mystery Babylon is an entirely different animal. This is the Whore in Revelation. Obviously, she encompasses the "confusion" of her earlier counterpart but also takes on the additional descriptive adjective: "Mystery." So, what is the "mystery" of Mystery Babylon?

If the original Babylon suggests or implies 'confusion,' then 'Mystery Babylon" would seem to suggest or imply not only 'confusion,' but also something not understood, unexplainable, or something that baffles; an enigma. The dictionary tells us that 'mystery' comes from the Greek word meaning 'secret rite,' 'to close the eyes,' or to 'initiate.' Is this what our 'masters' are doing with the deceptive use of words in our laws? Have they 'closed our eyes' to our true sovereign status, to our history and heritage? Have our laws become 'enigmas,' understood only by those who are 'initiated' into some manner of 'secret rite?'

But, Mystery Babylon is more than confusion; it is also INSANITY! Because her mysteries, her enigmas can, at times, drive people actually and literally insane. Look at how many people have committed suicide because of the IRS. You may hear of only a handful, but there have been many. Just a few years ago, one of ESPN's announcers shot himself to death because he had been convicted of failure to file income on his income tax returns, tax returns that, you will eventually discover, are and must be voluntary. As many of you already know, THIS IS INSANITY! Our traditional enemies actually love this! They are the masters of terror, fear and intimidation. Control of the herd by high-profile individuals, driven to suicide out of sheer desperation! What a form of control, intimidation and subtle tyranny!

In this publication, we will cover many of Mystery Babylon's tricks and techniques. This book is intended for all Americans, but is ESPECIALLY designed for those of you who have just awoken to the dreadful state of affairs in our great Nation, as you discover the traitorous activities of our **AGENTS OF GOVERNMENT** on 911. You unfortunate people have awoken from a really bad dream only to find out that you're right smack in the middle of an unbelievably real NIGHTMARE!

Before I show you the techniques they use to dumb us down, let's see what the Bible says about it. There is a very telling verse in the Book of James: "***a double- minded man is uncertain in all his ways!***" Don't you think the word "uncertain" could easily mean "confusion?" "Mystery Babylon" with the mystery taken out and explained? Be your own judge; I have already made up my mind.

Let's look at what I like to call the "knot-tying technique" used by Mystery Babylon. This will illustrate the use of the technique as it is set up and used against us with a very timely example.

Imagine that it's 1960, and you see me come up to an old friend, Jeff, whom I hadn't seen in some time, and you heard these words come forth from my mouth: "Jeff, it's so great to see you! It makes me 'gay'!" On a separate occasion, you and I might be going to a gala party and we might both describe it as "a gay event." What would you think? Would that word, 'gay' have a different connotation today as opposed to its meaning in 1960? The intervening decades have established a meaning and usage unknown in 1960. These may be silly examples, but I'm sure you get the idea: words can, and do, take on different meanings over time and with usage.

What they've done is to take the word 'gay,' that, for its entire previous existence, had always had a very positive definition and connotation, and coupled it, by modern usage, with something that a large majority of people find morally disgusting, repugnant and repulsive. They take a word that had previously possessed a long-established, positive connotation, and ascribe to it a new and distasteful connotation. In other words, your subconscious immediately associates the already-established positive definition with the new usage of the word, literally changing, in your subconscious, the distaste and revulsion you would ordinarily have associated with the homosexual lifestyle. Because the subconscious mind works faster than the conscious mind, this newer, more positive connotation and definition takes control before your slower-reacting conscious mind can totally rule it out. Then they start hammering us with it. Beginning more than ten years ago, this new 'definition' kicked in, and now it's used and reinforced constantly. I don't watch network TV shows nor do I own a television, but I know that there are many, MANY homosexual characters in today's sitcoms and movies. These programs and movies constantly hammer that word into your subconscious: he's gay, she's gay, gay marriage, gay rights, gay day, gay parades, gay, gay, gay!!! Over time and with usage, the previous connotation is practically obliterated and the newer definition takes effect. Opposites, opposites, opposites! ALWAYS look 180 degrees in the opposite direction to whatever it is they are trying to trick or condition you with.

What did the Rabbi say? "All they have to hear is the word 'defense' and they quit thinking!"

Now, you've had the term 'gay,' wrapped up in a positive connotation, shoved into your subconscious, until most, if not ALL, revulsion you might have previously experienced is neutralized. This is a major technique I've come to understand of Mystery Babylon!

Now, let's look at another example whereby opposite meanings are ascribed to words at the whim of the powers that be. This example 'really' shows the confusion of Mystery Babylon.

For years I would carry a 1995 'walking liberty' U.S. silver dollar. I carried it in my pocket and would use this little example with as many people as I could find who would listen. In 2011, I still have that silver eagle and still do this demonstration, even here in Argentina.

I would pull out the silver dollar while at a store while paying for a purchase or just talking with someone. If in a store, I would be sure to drop it on the counter. Those of you who have played with silver dollars know that it makes a really pleasant sound very different from the copper-nickel coins supplied to us today. Bystanders will usually say something like, "Wow! I'll bet that's old!" "Not really," I would say, handing it to them. "What's the date on it?" I'd ask. With a quizzical look on their face, they reply, "1995!" And now, they have a definite confused look. "You didn't know they were minting these?" I'd ask. "You can thank Representative Ron Paul for that one; he personally walked that bill through Congress," I would tell them. "Now, what does it say on the back?" They turn it over and look and read, "United States of America, 1 oz. fine silver, one dollar."

Now, I proceed to lock down what they've told me, "So it says, United States of America, 1 oz. Fine silver, one dollar and the date is 1995. "Is that correct?" "Yes," they always reply. At this point, I have found it important that they actually hold that silver dollar in one of their hands. Now I hand them a "**F**"ederal "**R**"eserve "**A**"ccounting "**U**"nit "**D**"ollar, or ***FRAUD***. I always say, "You've seen one or two of these, I'll bet!" "Of course," they always reply. Now I ask, "Can you read to me what it says in big letters on the front. "United States of America," at the top and "One Dollar," at the bottom. Now, you've got them with the silver dollar in one hand and the FRAUD in the other. "They both say United States of America, they both say one dollar, and you'll have to take my word on this, they both come from the United States Mint, Bureau of Printing and Engraving, is that correct?" "Yep," they answer. As they hold the silver eagle in one hand and the FRAUD in the other hand, I ask, "If that's correct, why does it take 10 of these one dollar bills to buy one of these silver dollars?" "Because it's made of silver?" they would ask occasionally. "Not at all," I'd answer. "It states clearly that it's one dollar. Different societies have used all kinds of things as money such as tobacco, seashells and many other items at one time or another. It doesn't matter what it is; it matters what it says it is, and this says it's one dollar."

(You can easily see that was an old example, because today it would take at least 45 of those FRAUDS to buy just one Silver Eagle. That is if you are lucky enough to find one to buy!)

If you want to see Mystery Babylon's confusion live and in person, you should see the looks on people's faces! Their looks are really priceless after this demonstration! Now they're faced with the dialectic right in their own hands. Usually, they will just recognize one side of this exercise and ignore the other side, because we have all been conditioned to understand the term 'money' to mean something of 'value,' 'substance' or 'worth,' when the truth is exactly the polar and total opposite. Today's 'money' is nothing but 'debt.' Remember the rule: look 180 degrees in the opposite direction for the real truth!

They've gotten an entire society not only calling, BUT BELIEVING that, today's 'money' represents a store of wealth and something positive. The sad truth is that it actually represents 'debt' and is, therefore, something totally destructive and extremely negative! This simple demonstration really confuses people, but it can help to untie the knots created in their minds. At that point, I will usually say, "Does the phrase 'unequal weights and measures' mean anything to you?" It doesn't matter whether I gave a detailed explanation or if I just used that simple phrase; I tried always to end this little exercise with a question about 'unequal weights and measures.' "Sure" they say. "Well, that's obviously what you have here." Then, I close with this statement," "If you ever find out why it takes 50 of those to buy one of these, you'll have a good idea of what's wrong with the country."

If, at that point, they were truly interested, I would usually tell them to acquire and read *The Creature From Jekyll Island* by G. Edward Griffin.

This is a very hard-hitting example to use with people, because both of these conflicting concepts are in the conscious part of their mind and they create total cognitive dissonance.

These examples are much more appropriate for those people who have awoken from what they very often consider to have been a bad dream turned into a terrible nightmare! Consider, for example, the complicity of Agents of Government in the events of 911. Now that you're awake, you're starting to see all these 'word-knots' that have been tied in your mind. You have these two totally and completely different meanings being associated with the same word. To me, this IS Mystery Babylon, not only defined, but explained!

You now have a tool to help you deal with the confusion they intentionally purvey to the masses. These demons know very well, and understand much better than we do, the Biblical and historical examples they have put into practical application. They are quite aware that *"a double minded man is uncertain in all his ways."*

Here's yet another word that is extremely topical these days: "terrorist." listen to their chatter with that word: "terrorists want to attack us because we're so free!" "They attacked you because they hate your freedoms!" The very first definition of "terrorism" in the Oxford English Dictionary is "Intimidation by government..." Seems pretty straightforward to me. No 180-degree definition in that word, is there?

Perhaps you're starting to see what they're doing. Yes, "the (real) terrorists DO hate your freedoms!" And the REAL "terrorists" have had a field day, taking away one freedom after another, especially since 911. The Patriot Act, for example, was a collection of laws that the FBI had hoped to pass for years, but could never get the necessary votes in Congress to have them enacted. After 911, the FBI lawyers beat a hasty path to Congress with their proposed legislation and included therein every manner of classic word-twisting they could manage!

The lies and perversions don't stop with the passage of such legislation. To achieve maximum effectiveness requires education of the public, government propaganda, if you will. They tie your mind in additional knots by proclaiming that, "If you're not with us, you're with the terrorists!" This slogan originated in Communist Russia during the 1930s. It worked then, and the phrase and technique is working again, just as it always has in the past! That is, UNLESS you understand the game that is being played. Once you fully grasp their agenda and their techniques, they and their actions become as transparent as looking "Through the Looking Glass."

We'll get into their word-games and twisting of the law in much greater depth in the following pages.

~ WHY DON'T AMERICANS DO SOMETHING? ~

The term "False Flag" comes from the days of piracy on the high seas. The pirate ship would fly the flag of a friendly county. When the targeted ship would approach and get so close enough that it could no longer change its course, the pirate ship would lower the "false flag" and run up the skull and crossbones, the so-called Jolly Roger!

There are those who believe that federal agents were involved in the tragic events that occurred in the bombing of the Alfred E. Murrah building in Oklahoma City in 1995. They believe that these agents "False Flagged" the incident in the "heartland of America." Fortunately, not long after the bombing, Brigadier General Benton Parton, U.S.A.F. (Ret.), a true patriot, stepped forward publicly to reveal the true facts behind this tragedy. During his Air Force career, he was the original officer in charge of setting up an Air Force department called the Weapons System Division. General Parton formed this new division of the Air Force from scratch. He was given no building, no file cabinets, nothing but the assignment to accomplish. Having the responsibility of looking 25 to 50 years into the future, General Parton had to attempt to conceive exactly 'whom' we would probably be fighting.

At that time, the opposing political and military system most likely to threaten America was Communism. So, he became an ardent student of Communism and eventually was recognized as one of the leading experts in the country on that particular form of tyrannical government. His research has many implications, but the following excerpt from his talk struck yet another chord with me. I've never forgotten it and have always felt that this is an important part of the Communist puzzle; it gave me an insight into how they plan and execute their schemes at home and abroad. In his excellent talk on Communism and the 1929 White Paper of the Communist International, General Parton stated, *"When we were studying Freud, they were studying Pavlov!"*

This is the part that turned a couple of floodlights on for me. Here are all three stages of the Pavlovian (conditioned-response) experiments that many of us have been taught about in school. However, they only exposed us to the first stage.

- The first stage was the one taught in our schools. Pavlov gave his dog food and rang a bell simultaneously. Eventually, he could ring the bell without the food, and the dogs would salivate.

- In the second stage, he used the same dog in a room but conditioned the dog to turn on the light, after which Pavlov would beat the dog with a stick. The dog could only escape the beating by running to the corner and diving under a board parallel to the floor.

- In the third stage, Pavlov took the same dog in the same room. He rang the bell and turned on the light at the same time. What do you think the dog did?

Most people say that he salivated and dove under the board at the same time. Of course, that seems like the logical answer. Actually, the dog stood in the middle of the room and shook. Psychologists today call that a "catatonic state."

This, I firmly believe, is why most Americans do NOTHING!

They're locked into their television and are getting contradictory messages that are DESIGNED to induce a catatonic state. Television, of course, has additional hypnotizing effects. Like the dog in the third stage of Pavlov's famous experiments, they just sit there and shake, some mentally, others physically. I hope you will give some serious thought to this concept and its application in today's world.

Recently I heard an EXCELLENT interview with a Dr. Bruce Lipton on The Power Hour. In fact, Joyce Riley, the moderator, stated that Dr. Lipton was the program's 3rd MOST REQUESTED GUEST! Dr. Lipton has some totally fascinating material, but two things that he said just made the hair on my arm stand straight up!

First, he stated that our subconscious mind runs our lives 95% of the day. That's a tremendous piece of information; it explains how the powers that be use "knot- tying," explained above, in their agenda.

Second, he stated that, when people get their conscious and subconscious working together, it is EMPOWERING! Once again, that is what we will be doing in this short exposé – empowering you, hopefully, by showing you how to merge the thoughts in your conscious and subconscious to empower yourself against an enemy using such deceptive and effective tactics that are very difficult to discern. I hope to enable you to identify the tactics that are being used against not only you but against the entire world.

Let's look at another more recent example of subconscious manipulation. The first Monday after the recent CSPAN broadcast on 911, some of us heard all the "talking heads," (Sean Hannity & Mossad Michael Medved, et al.). Personally, I have a difficult time listening to all of these puppets, these talking heads.   Why?

Because (like Victor Marsden who was the original translator of *The Protocols of the Learned Elders of Zion*, who could only work on the translation for 30 minutes at a time without becoming physically sick), I can only stand listening to them for short periods of time without getting physically and mentally sick. But I digress. The ones I heard addressing the callers would all state, in a chant-like cadence, "we all saw the planes fly into the buildings," "we all saw the planes fly into the buildings," "we ALL saw the planes fly into the buildings!" Conditioning 101!

I can guarantee you that whoever put out those talking points had a deep understanding of subconscious suggestion and programming and their effects. Unfortunately, many Americans, being willing members of the servile state, buy into that technique without questioning it or even thinking about it. This is a perfect example of subconscious mind control.

I found myself yelling at the radio, "I saw David Copperfield make the Statue of Liberty AND a plane disappear!" "I saw it with my own eyes!"

When you fully wake up and you've had the opportunity to clear the intentionally placed cobwebs in your mind, you will scream, "The emperor has NO clothes!" Their game will become totally exposed and almost sophomoric, if not for the disastrous consequences of their rules!

~ HOW LAWS ARE MADE ~
How Laws are made: Bills are originated in either the House of Representatives (HR) or in the Senate (S). After both sides of Congress pass a piece of legislation, they convene in a "conference committee" if there are major differences in their respective pieces of legislation. They hammer out a compromise, and the final Bill is

then sent to the President for his signature. After it is signed, the legislation is then passed to the federal agency that is responsible for its administration and enforcement. The appropriate agency then promulgates regulations that state EXACTLY who the legislation is enforced upon. There are three different types of regulations but ONLY ONE type that applies directly to the 'public,' namely, "Substantive Regulations." Before this type of regulation takes legal effect, it must go through a very, VERY specific type of promulgation process named "Notice & Comment." If those regulations are not promulgated EXACTLY as required by the notice and comment procedure, they are null, void and indefensible in a court. You can defeat them on procedural technicalities by bringing up the technicality that was not adhered to or followed.

This is important for several reasons. We will refer to this procedure several times, so it's important that you understand how it's done. Most likely, you have never been exposed to the law-making process. As the old saying goes, "sausage and laws are two things you do not want to see made!"

For one thing, anyone who has ever dealt with federal regulations knows how complex and confusing they can be. Not only are they complicated to read, they are complicated to promulgate by the particular federal agency that is responsible for their enforcement. This process takes literally months not only to write or draft the original regulation, but also to put the proposed regulation through the specific procedures required by law in the Administrative Procedures Act (APA).

I remember hearing, at one point, that the complete set of NAFTA regulations was entered in the Federal Register the day following the signing by Bill Clinton. Someone can easily

check that if you'd care to. I never have, but it would conform perfectly with the way these traitors set their agenda up and do things.

Quoted from the Declaration of Independence:

> *"He has erected a multitude of New Offices, and sent other swarms of Officers to harass our people, and eat out their substance."*

Sound familiar? This is not 'almost' exactly what is going on today, but precisely what is going on. As the Spanish philosopher George Santayana said many years ago, *"**those who do not learn their lessons from history are destined to repeat them.**"*

PART III

"[I]f the public are bound to yield obedience to laws to which they cannot give their approbation, they are slaves to those who make such laws and enforce them." - Candidus, in *the Boston Gazette*, 1772

VOICES AND WISDOM - SPEAKING FROM HISTORY

No man escapes when freedom fails, The best men rot in filthy jails, And those who cried "Appease! Appease!" Are hanged by those they tried to please. - **Anonymous**

"Woe unto you, lawyers! For ye have taken way the key of knowledge: ye entered not in yourselves, and them that were entering in ye hindered." - **Gospel of Luke**. XI, 5

"There are none so helplessly enslaved as those who falsely believe they are free." - **Goethe**.

"The 1st engine of tyranny is a corrupt judiciary." – Famous English jurist.

"A double minded man is uncertain in ALL of his ways." - **Book of James 1:8, Bible**.

"When I use a word," Humpty Dumpty said, in a rather scornful tone, *"it means just what I choose it to mean – no more no less."* *"The question is*," said Alice, *"whether you can make words mean so many different things."* *"The question is*," said Humpty Dumpty, *"which is to be master – that's all."* - Alice In Wonderland, **Lewis Carroll**.

"Extremism in defense of liberty is NO vice." – **Barry Goldwater.**

"Those who don't learn their lessons from history are destined to repeat them." - **George Santayana**

"The worst thing that could happen to America is the two-party system." **John Adams**, Founding Father

"A nation can survive its fools, and even the ambitious. But it cannot survive treason from within. An enemy at the gates is less formidable, for he is known and he carries his banners openly. But the traitor moves among those within the gate freely, his sly whispers rustling through all the galleys, heard in the very hall of government itself. For the traitor appears not traitor – he speaks in the accents familiar to his victims, and wears their face and their garments, and he appeals to the baseness that lies deep in the hearts of all men. He rots the soul of a nation – he works secretly and unknown in the night to undermine the pillars of a city – he infects the body politic so that it can no longer resist. A murderer is less to be feared." - **Marcus Tullius Cicero**, 106-42 B.C.

"If man, through fear, fraud, or mistake, should in terms renounce or give up any natural right, the eternal law of reason and the grand end of society would absolutely vacate such renunciation. The right to freedom being the gift of God, it is not in the power of man to alienate this gift and voluntarily become a slave." - **Samuel Adams**, Father of the American Revolution

"I have never been able to conceive how any rational being could propose happiness to himself from the exercise of power over others." - **Thomas Jefferson**

"No man is good enough to govern another man without that other's consent." - **Abraham Lincoln**

"Power and law are not synonymous. In truth, they are frequently in opposition and irreconcilable. There is God's Law from which all equitable laws of man emerge and by which men must live if they are not to die in oppression, chaos and despair. Divorced from God's eternal and immutable Law, established before the founding of the suns, man's power is evil no matter the noble words with which it is employed or the motives urged when enforcing it. Men of good will, mindful therefore of the Law laid down by God, will oppose governments whose rule is by men, and if they wish to survive as a nation they will destroy the government which attempts to adjudicate by the whim of venal judges." - **Marcus Tullius Cicero**, 106-43 B.C.

"I love America more than any other country in this world; and, exactly for this reason, I insist on the right to criticize her perpetually." - **James Baldwin**

"How little do my countrymen know what precious blessings they are in possession of, and which __NO__ other people on earth enjoy!" - **Thomas Jefferson** (emphasis added)

"If you love wealth more than Liberty, the tranquility of servitude better than the animating contest of Freedom, depart from us in peace. We ask not your counsel nor your arms. Crouch down and lick the hand that feeds you. May your chains rest lightly upon you and may posterity forget that you were our countrymen." - **Samuel Adams**

"To sin by silence when they should protest makes cowards of men." - **Abraham Lincoln**

"Nothing in the world can take the place of persistence. Talent will not: nothing is more common that unsuccessful men with talent. Genius will not: unrewarded genius is almost a proverb. Education alone will not: the world is full of educated derelicts. Persistence and determination alone are omnipotent." - **Calvin Coolidge**

"It is not the critic who counts, not the man who points out how the strong man stumbled or where the doer of deeds could have done them better. The credit belongs to the man who is actually in the arena; whose face is marred by dust and sweat and blood; who strives valiantly; who errs and comes short again and again; who knows the great enthusiasms, the great devotions, and spends himself in a worthy cause; who, at best, knows the triumph of high achievement, and who, at the worst, if he fails, at least fails while daring greatly, so that his place shall never be with those cold and timid souls who know neither victory nor defeat." - **Theodore Roosevelt**, April 23, 1917

"The right is more precious than peace." - **Woodrow Wilson**

"We have enjoyed so much freedom for so long that we are perhaps in danger of forgetting how much blood it cost to establish the Bill of Rights." - **Felix Frankfurter**

"Indeed, I tremble for my country when I reflect that God is just." - **Thomas Jefferson**

"It's getting more and more difficult to support the government in the style to which it has become accustomed." - **Will Rogers** (I believe)

"A little rebellion now and then is a good thing, and as necessary in the political world as storms in the physical." - **Thomas Jefferson**

"As long as our government is administered for the good of the people and is regulated by their will, it will be worth defending." - **Andrew Jackson** 1829-1837

"The world is governed by far different persons that what is imagined by those not behind the scenes." - **Benjamin Disraeli**

"Because of what appears to be a lawful command on the surface, many citizens, because of their respect for what only appears to be law, are cunningly coerced into waiving their rights due to ignorance." - U.S. v. Minker, 350 U.S. 179, 187 (1956).

~ QUOTES ON MONEY ~

"We have stricken the (slave) shackles from four million human beings and brought all laborers to a common level, not so much by the elevation of former slaves as by practically reducing the whole working population, white and black, to a condition of serfdom. While boasting of our noble deeds, we are careful to conceal the ugly fact that by our iniquitous money system we have nationalized a system of oppression which, though more refined, is no less cruel than the old system of chattel slavery."
- Horace Greeley

"The few who can understand the system (checks, money and credits) will either be so interested in its profits, or so dependent on its favors, that there will be no opposition from that class, while on the other hand, the great body of the people mentally incapable of comprehending the tremendous advantage that capital derives from the system, will bear its burdens without complaint, and perhaps without even suspecting that the system is inimical to their interests." - **Rothschild Brothers of London**

The London Times printed the following paragraph during our Civil War:

"If that mischievous financial policy, which had its origin in the North American Republic should become indurated down to a fixture, then that Government will furnish its own money without cost. It will pay off debts and be without a debt. It will have all the money necessary to carry on its commerce. It will become prosperous beyond precedent in the history of the civilized governments

of the world. The brains and the wealth of all countries will go to North America. That government must be destroyed or it will destroy every monarchy on the globe. They will not hesitate to plunge the whole of Christendom into wars and chaos in order that the earth should become their inheritance." - Said to have been published as a *London Times* editorial (1865).

"My agency in promoting the passage of the National Bank Act was the greatest financial mistake of my life. It has built up a monopoly which affects every interest in the country. It should be repealed; but before that can be accomplished, the people will be arrayed on one side and the banks on the other, in a contest such as we have never seen before in this country." - **Salmon P. Chase**

"The money power preys upon the nation in times of peace, and conspires against it in times of adversity. It is more despotic than monarchy, more insolent than autocracy, more selfish than bureaucracy. It denounces, as public enemies, all who question its methods or throw light upon its crimes." - **Abraham Lincoln**

"I believe that banking institutions are more dangerous to our liberties than standing armies. Already they have raised up a moneyed aristocracy that has set the Government at defiance. The issuing power should be taken from the banks restored to the people to whom it properly belongs." - **President Thomas Jefferson** (attributed).

"Whoever controls the volume of money in any country is absolute master of all industry and commerce." - **President James A. Garfield**

"The only honest dollar is a dollar of stable, debt-paying, purchasing power. The only honest dollar is a dollar which repays the creditor the value he lent and no more, and requires the debtor to pay the value borrowed and no more." - **Senator Robert L. Owen**, (Okla.) 1913

"I had never thought the Federal Bank System would prove such a failure. The country is in a state of irretrievable bankruptcy." - **Senator Carter Glass**, June 7, 1938

(These two previous quotes were from United States Senators responsible for the initiation and enactment of the Federal Reserve Act of 1913.)

"If the American people ever allow private banks to control the issue of their currency, first by inflation and then deflation, the banks and corporations that will grow up around them will deprive the people of all property until their children will wake up homeless on the continent their fathers conquered." - **Thomas Jefferson** (attributed).

"Banking was conceived in iniquity and born in sin. Bankers own the earth. Take it away from them but leave them the power to create money and, with the flick of the pen, they will create enough money to buy it back again. Take this great power away from them and all great fortunes like mine will disappear and they ought to disappear, for then this would be a better and happier world to live in. But, if you want to continue to be slaves of the bankers and pay the

cost of your own slavery, then let bankers continue to create money and control credit." - **Sir Joseph Stamp**, President, Bank of England

"I see in the near future a crisis approaching that unnerves me, and causes me to tremble for the future of my country; corporations will follow, and the money power of the country will endeavor to prolong its reign by working upon the prejudices of the people, until the wealth is aggregated in a few hands, and the Republic [note, **not** "Democracy"] *destroyed."* - **Abraham Lincoln**

"It is well enough that people of the nation do not understand our banking and monetary system, for if they did, I believe there would be a revolution before tomorrow morning." - **Henry Ford, Sr.**

"The youth who can solve the money question will do more for the world than all the professional soldiers of history." - **Henry Ford, Sr.**

"The only dynamite that works in this country is the dynamite of a sound idea. I think we are getting a sound idea on the money question. The people have an instinct which tells them that something is wrong and that the wrong somehow centers in money.

Don't allow them to confuse you with the cry of 'paper money.' The danger of paper money is precisely the danger of gold – if you get too much it is no good. There is just one rule for money and that is to have enough to carry all the legitimate trade that is waiting to move. Too little and too much are both bad. But enough to move trade, enough to prevent stagnation on the one hand, not enough to permit speculation on the other hand, is the proper ratio.

If our country can issue a dollar bond, it can issue a dollar bill. The element that makes the bond good, makes the bill good also. The difference between the bond and the bill is that the bond lets money brokers collect the amount of the bond and an additional 20 percent interest, whereas the currency pays nobody but those who contribute directly in some useful way.

It is absurd to say that our country can issue $30,000,000 in bonds and not $30,000,000 in currency. Both are promises to pay; but one promise fattens the usurer and the other helps the people.

It is the people who constitute the basis of government credit. Why then cannot the people have benefit of their own gilt-edge credit by receiving non-interest-bearing currency – instead of bankers receiving the benefit of the people's credit in interest- bearing bonds? If the United States Government will adopt this policy of increasing its national wealth without contributing to the interest collector – for the whole national debt is made up on interest charges – then you will see an era of progress and prosperity in this country such as could never have come otherwise." - **Thomas A. Edison**

"Capital must protect itself in every way, through combination and through legislation. Debts must be collected and loans and mortgages foreclosed as soon as possible. When, through a process of law, the common people lost their homes, they will be more tractable and more easily governed by the strong arm of the law, applied by the central power of wealth, under control of leading financiers. People without homes will not quarrel with their leaders. This is well known among our principal men

> *now engaged in forming an imperialism of capital to govern the world. **<u>By dividing the people, we can get them to expend their energies in fighting over questions of no importance to us except as teachers of the common herd</u>**. Thus, by discreet action we can secure for ourselves what has been generally planned and successfully accomplished."* - Printed from ***the Banker's Manifest***, for private circulation among leading bankers only. *"Civil Servants' Year Book* (The Organizer)" January 1934 & "New American" February 1934. (emphasis added)

The Duke of Bedford, realizing the enormity of the sellout of the International Bankers, made the following remarks before the House of Lords on December 17, 1945, at the time the Bretton Woods proposal was before the British Government:

> *"I find that opposition to the Bretton Woods scheme, which is one of the conditions of the loan, is almost universal among people of widely different political and economic outlook . . . I find that the really fine and enlightened people of America are as much against Bretton Woods and all that it stands for as I am.*
>
> *Then there is the very grave objection indeed that WE ARE PROPOSING TO HAND OVER THE CONTROL OF OUR ECONOMIC LIFE, in a very large measure, to a gang of representatives of Wall Street finance who are responsible to no one and are above every Government."* - **Duke of Bedford**, American Mercury, April 1957, p. 137.
>
> *"I believe that if the people of this nation fully understood what Congress has done to them over the last 49 years, they would move on Washington; they*

would not wait for an election. It adds up to a preconceived plan to destroy the economic and social independence of the United States!" - **Senator George W. Malone** (Nevada) Speaking before Congress 1957

"If all the bank loans were paid, no one would have a bank deposit and there would not be a dollar of coin or currency in circulation. This is a staggering thought.

We are completely dependent on the commercial banks. Someone has to borrow every dollar we have in circulation. ***If the banks create ample synthetic money****, we are prosperous; if not, we starve. We are absolutely without a permanent money system. When one gets a complete grasp of the picture, the tragic absurdity of our hopeless position is almost incredible, but there it is.* ***It (the banking problem) is the most important subject intelligent persons can investigate and reflect upon. It is so important that our present civilization may collapse unless it becomes widely understood and the defects remedied very soon.*** *"* - **U.S. Senate document** #23, page102, 1/24/39, **Mr. Robert Hemphill**, for 8 years Credit Manager of the Federal Reserve Bank of Atlanta. (Emphasis added)

~ LEGAL DEFINITIONS ~

Law: Rights + Duties = Remedies. Secures to one person a right, ascribes the duty to other persons to respect the right(s) secured, and provides a remedy to the secured person when the right has been violated.

Person: *A being or entity, natural or artificial, to which the law ascribes rights or duties.*

> *"Persons are the subject of rights and duties; and, as a subject of a right, the person is the object of a correlative duty, and conversely. The subject of a right has been called by Professor Holland, the person of inherence; the subject of a duty, the person of incidence. "Entitled" and "bound" are the terms in common use in English and for most purposes they are adequate. Every full citizen is a person; other human beings, namely, subjects who are not citizens, may be persons. But not every human being is necessarily a person, for a person is capable of rights and duties and there may well be human beings having no legal rights, __as was the case with slaves (feudal serfs) in English law__. It includes women."* - Bouvier's Law Dictionary, p. 2575 (1914).

Scope and delineation of the term [person] is necessary for determining those to whom Fourteenth Amendment of Constitution affords protection since this Amendment expressly applies to a "person." *Black's Law Dictionary*, 6th Edition

> **Liberty**: *Right of locomotion* (Blackstone's Commentaries) (*The ability to go from point A to point B unimpeded*).

Status: *The status of an individual, used as a legal term, means the legal position of the individual in or with regard to the rest of the community. L.R. 4 P.D.11. The rights, duties, capacities and incapacities which determine a person to a given class, constitute his status; Campb. Austin 137. It also means estate, because it signifies the condition or circumstances in which one stands with regard to his property . . .* Pollack and Maitland, Hist. E.L. 11.

Resident: Political or geographic term? Exactly WHICH body of law covers you? Pertinent legal definition comes from "Minister" in Governmental Law. - Bouvier's Law Dictionary, 1914.

Residence: (a) *The act or fact of dwelling in a place for some time.* (b) *The act or fact of living or regularly staying at or in some **place for the discharge of a duty or the enjoyment of a benefit**.*
Merriam- webster.com/dictionary/residence

Property: *Actually a right. A person's right of ownership in or to a thing.*

Ownership: *The right to the possession and use of a thing to the exclusion of all others.*

Thing: *A determinate object to which the law recognizes a person may have a right.* **To turn a thing into a person is a feat that can not be performed without the aid of the state.** Pollack & Maitland, p. 18.

Subject: *A being or entity that is politically subject to a particular law or jurisdiction.*

Contract: *An agreement between two or more parties to do or not to do a particular thing.*

Jurisdiction: *The power and authority, constitutionally conferred, by which courts and judicial officers take cognizance of and decide cases according to law, and it governs the legal right by which the court can exercise its authority. Without it, a court's pronouncements are void.*

License: (In Real Property Law) A permission. A right given by some competent authority to do an act, without which such authority would be illegal, or a tort or trespass. A permission to do some act or series of acts on the land of the licensor, without having any permanent interest in it . . . *Morrill v. Mackman*, 24 Mich., 282. Bouvier's Law Dictionary, 1914. The permission by competent authority to do an act which, without such permission, would be illegal, a trespass, a tort, or otherwise not allowable. *People v. Henderson*, 391 Mich. 612. A permit, granted by an appropriate governmental body, generally for a consideration, to a person, firm or corporation to pursue some occupation or to carry on some business subject to regulation under the police powers . . . *Rosenblatt v. California State Board of Pharmacy*, 69 Cal.App.2d 69, 158. Blacks Law Dictionary, Sixth Edition. Certificate or the document itself which gives permission. *Aldrich v. City of Syracuse*, 236 N.Y.S. 614, 617. Black's Law Dictionary, Revised Fourth Edition.

Terrorism: *Intimidation by government . . .* Oxford English Dictionary

Citizen: *One who, under the Constitution and law of the United States, or of a particular state, is a member of the political community, **owing allegiance** and being entitled to the enjoyment of full **civil rights**. All persons born or naturalized in the United States, and subject to the jurisdiction thererof, are citizens of the United States and of the state wherein they reside.* U.S. Constitution 14th Amendment; see 'Citizenship,' Black's Law Dictionary, 6th Edition.

Citizenship: *The status of being a citizen. There are four ways to acquire citizenship: by birth in the United States, by birth in U.S. territories, by birth outside the U.S. to U.S. parents, and by naturalization.* - Black's Law Dictionary, 6th Edition.

citizen of the United States: *Literal 2nd class citizen under the scope and purview of the 14th Amendment, possessing only "civil rights" granted by government.*

Citizen Of The United States, **American** or **American or U.S. National**: *Original Sovereign Citizen. Recipient of Rights & Duties from the Creator, as set forth in the Declaration of Independence. In the tax code of the United States, 26 U.S.C. § 7701(b)(1)(B), this status is identified as a "non-resident alien."*

Slave: *One over whose life, liberty, and property another has unlimited control. The slave could not* *acquire property:* ***his acquisitions belonged to his master****: Jackson v. Lervey,* 5 Cow. (N.Y.) 397.

Slavery: "who owns your labor?" Which kind of slavery? There are at least two kinds to consider:

- Southern slavery

- Feudal system

The Unfree – denoted by various terms at different times: Lord Coke, in the 1650s, in his Institutes, called such a man a villein and a woman a knave.

Comyn, in his Digest, current at the time of the American Revolution, considered them under the appellation of copyholders. (A copyhold estate was originally an estate at the will of the lord.)

What do you think they are called today in American law? How about resident?

In rendering his oath of fealty to his lord, a villain was required to pledge: "*I will be justified by you in my body and goods.*" Just 'exactly' HOW free are we, really?

> "*In his treatment of the subject, Bracton frequently insists on the relativity of serfdom. Serfdom with him is hardly a status; it is but a relation between two persons: serf and lord. As regards his lord, the serf has, at least as a rule, no rights; but as regards other persons he has all or nearly all the rights of a free man; it is nothing to them that he is a serf.*" - **Pollock & Maitland**, p. 19a

"Slavery is like holding a wolf by the ears, you can't afford to hold him and you can't afford to let him go." - **Thomas Jefferson**

Servitude: In Civil Law: *The subjection of one person to another person or of a person to a thing, or of a thing to a person, or of a thing to a thing.*

A right which subjects a land or tenement to some service for the use of another land or tenement, which belongs to another master. Domat, Civ. Law, Cushing's ed. Sec.
1018.

A <u>mixed</u> servitude is the subjection of persons to things, or things to persons.

A <u>natural</u> servitude is one, which arises in consequence of the natural condition or situation of the soil.

A personal servitude is the subjection of one person to another: **<u>If it consists in the right of property which a person exercises over another, it is slavery.</u>** *When the subjection of one person to another is not slavery, it consists simply in the right of requiring of another what he is bound to do or not to do: this right arises from all kinds of contracts or quasi-contracts.* Lois des Bat. P.1, c.1, art. 1.

Servitus (Lat.): In Roman law. *Servitude: slavery; a state of bondage; a disposition of the law of nations by which, against common right, one man has been subjected to the dominion of another.* Inst 1. 2. 3; Bracton 4 b: Co. Litt. 116

Money: *Gold and Silver coins. The common medium of exchange in a civilized nation.* - Bovier's Law Dictionary (1914).

Dr. Bill Veeth's analysis asks, *"Has the value of an inch changed? Has the volume of a quart changed?"* Coinage Act of 1779, 371.25 grains of silver IS still, by operation of law, one Dollar.

United States: *"The term 'United States' may be used in any one of several senses. It may be merely the name of a sovereign occupying the position analogous to that of other sovereigns in the family of nations. It may designate the territory over which the sovereignty of the United States extends, or it may be the collective name of the states which are united by and under the Constitution." Hooven & Allison Co. v. Evatt*, 324 U.S. 652, 671-72 (1945).

Natural Person: *Individual, Rights and Duties in the same entity. Individual comes from indivisible Rights & Duties in Natural Person. A being that exists in nature.*

Artificial or Juristic Person: *An entity that does not exist in nature, but is the creation of law – a corporation, partnership, L.L.C., Trust, etc.*

De Jure: *Rightfully; of right; lawfully; by legal title.*

De Facto: *Actually; in fact; in deed. A term used to denote a thing actually done. An officer de facto is one who performs the duties of an office with apparent right, and under claim and color of an appointment, but without being actually qualified in law so to act.* <u>Brown v. Lunt</u>, *37 Me. 423. One who has the reputation of being the officer he assumes to be, and yet is not a good officer in point of law. 6 East 368. Bouvier's Law Dictionary,* 1914

Civil rights: *A term applied to certain rights secured to citizens of the United States by the 13th and 14th Amendments to the Constitution, and by various acts of congress made in pursuance thereof. - Bouvier's Law Dictionary 499 (1914).*

Political rights: *Pertaining to policy or the administration of the government. Political rights are those which may be exercised in the formation and administration of the government: they are distinguished from civil rights, which are the rights which a man enjoys as regards to other individuals, and not in relation to government. - Bouvier's Law Dictionary 2626 (1914).*

> *"Neither slavery nor involuntary servitude, except as a punishment for a crime, whereof the party shall have been duly convicted, shall exist within the United States, or any place subject to their jurisdiction."* - 13th Amendment.

Plural, *"their jurisdiction."* *"Voluntary servitude"* is left out and is, thereby, made legal by its omission. This deliberate omission was intended to allow for indentured servants and others who voluntarily wished to contract themselves or their children into a condition of servitude, etc. Constitutionally, the government cannot impair the right to contract. This is the loophole upon which our entire situation rests. I think we should be able to re-institute the original 13th Amendment that was taken off the books and hidden from the people. Those of you who may not have heard about this, briefly, the original 13th restricted lawyers from holding public office.

> *"All persons born or naturalized in the United States, and subject to the jurisdiction thereof, are citizens of the United States and the State wherein they reside."*
> - 14th Amendment.

From what we have already learned, there are five legal landmines in one sentence: person, United States, subject, jurisdiction, (and most important) resident. Also, notice the change of the term 'United States' to a singular entity!

You probably **DO NOT know** that *Bouvier*'s is the only Law Dictionary that is used in drafting laws for Congress. It has not been regularly printed since 1914.

~ Feudal and Allodial System ~

> *"Much of what has just been written pertains to almost prehistoric conditions. Since those times, two well-defined but very different types of land ownership have developed. Historically they are interesting and well worth fuller examination than the scope of this book permits. The feudal system conceived the absolute ownership of all land to be*

in the king or sovereign, the subject having merely a feud or right to use the land in return for services. The allodial system, on the other hand, recognized the principle that land might be owned by an individual, subject to no proprietary control of the sovereign. Both of these systems existed in England. When the United States was settled, the theory of the allodial system was the one on which our law of real property was based. The allodial system is the result of the breakdown of the feudal system, which left its mark on our theory of real property ownership. <u>This is evidenced by such heritages as the right of the state to impose taxes, to exercise its police power, and the right to escheat.</u>" - Real Estate Principles and Practices, Alfred A. Ring, 1972 (7th ed.)

~ Government limitations on ownership ~

The allodial system, although free of the "feuds," "services" or "duties" of the feudal system, did, nevertheless, impose certain political, rather than proprietary, obligations on the landowner. The owner was required to repair bridges, roads, and fortresses. In this country, landowners have duties and inescapable limitations on ownership and which are enforced by the government for the mutual welfare of the community. Among these are:

- Police power of the government
- Eminent domain
- Right to taxation
- Escheat to the state

Source: Real Estate Principles and Practices, Alfred A. Ring, 1972 (7th ed.)

~ Legal Maxims ~

"If you receive the benefit, you owe the duty." Legal maxim

> *Fraud is using deception in order to induce another to part with property or surrender some legal right and the parting with property or surrendering some legal right occurs. Fraud vitiates all contracts, written or verbal, sealed or unsealed.* - Landmark Dev. Group v. <u>Tmk Assocs.</u>, 2002 Conn. Super. LEXIS 731 (Conn. Super. Ct. Mar. 5, 2002).

> *If an assignment is obtained through some kind of fraud, the entire assignment is invalid. Fraud destroys the validity of everything into which it enters. It vitiates the most solemn contracts, documents, and even judgments.* - <u>International Milling Co.</u> v. <u>Priem</u>, 179 Wis. 622 (Wis. 1923).

Slaves CANNOT OWN PROPERTY! <u>They ARE property</u> and the object of someone else's property rights...

> *"It has been well and truly said that laws are not always promulgated for the benefit of the People. In Japan, for instance, down to the year 1870, laws were addressed only to the officials whose duty it would be to administer them in accordance with the Chinese maxim 'let the people abide by, but not be appraised of, the law.' N. Hozumi on the New Japanese Civil Code 1904."* - **Holland**, Jurisprudence, p. 40, n. 2 Tenth Edition (1908)

Words are the indispensable tools in understanding the concepts of either "freedom" or "tyranny." - James Wilson, signer of the Declaration, the Constitution and a justice on the first U.S. Supreme Court, tells us that each American, in international law, has the same rights as the Crown of England or any other sovereign. *The Works of James Wilson*

The definition for 'Common Law' in Cowell's Dictionary – the first English law dictionary – being *"Our most precious hereditament."*

> *"Gaius (Roman credited with the origination of law) knew . . . that all rights belong to persons, and that all law is addressed to persons: that a thing is always the object of a right, and cannot be reached by law, except through the medium of a person: and that a law (or right) would be of little avail if not furnished with a remedy, or action, in the broadest sense of the word."* - Hammond, *Introduction to Sander's Justinian*, American Edition p. 35 (1875)

~ **Case Cites** ~

The Slaughter-House Cases: 83 U.S. 36 (1873), was the first case wherein the U. S. Supreme Court interpreted the relatively new Fourteenth Amendment to the Constitution. It is viewed as a pivotal case in early civil rights law, reading the Fourteenth Amendment as protecting the "privileges or immunities" conferred by virtue of the federal United States citizenship to all individuals of all states within it, but not those privileges or immunities incident to citizenship of a state.

Properly known as *Slaughter-House Cases,* the decision consolidated three similar cases.

This is called the "benchmark" or "landmark" case on the 14th Amendment. *Slaughter-House* still stands as "good law" today, never having been overturned or overruled. After the state of Louisiana passed a law regulating slaughter houses, numerous butchers in the New Orleans area filed suits against the legislation. There were so many cases that the court lumped them all together, hence, the plural nomenclature.

~ **Background** ~

Facts of the Case: Louisiana had created a partial monopoly of the slaughtering business and gave it to one company.

Competitors argued that this created "involuntary servitude," abridged "privileges and immunities," denied "equal protection of the laws," and deprived them of "liberty and property without due process of law."

Question: Did the creation of the monopoly violate the Thirteenth and Fourteenth Amendments?

Conclusion: No. The involuntary servitude claim did not forbid limits on the right to use one's property. The equal protection claim was misplaced since it was established to void laws discriminating against blacks. The due process claim simply imposes the identical requirements on the states as the Fifth Amendment imposes on the national government. **The Court devoted most of its opinion to a narrow construction of the privileges and immunities clause, which was interpreted to apply to the newly created federal citizenship and 'not' the already existing state citizenship.**

>From the syllabus of the case, we read:
>> ***The first clause of the fourteenth article was primarily intended to confer citizenship on the negro race***, *and secondly to give definitions of citizenship of the United States and citizenship of the States, and it recognizes the distinction between citizenship of a State and citizenship of the United States by those definitions.*

Now, we read from the decision itself:
> *The process of restoring to their proper relations with the Federal government and with the other States those which had sided with the rebellion, undertaken under the proclamation of President Johnson in 1865 and before the assembling of Congress, developed the fact that, notwithstanding the formal recognition by those States of the abolition of slavery, the condition of the slave race would, without further protection of the Federal government, be almost as bad as it was before. Among the first acts of legislation adopted by several of the States in the legislative bodies which claimed to be in their normal relations with the Federal government were laws which imposed upon the colored race onerous disabilities and burdens and curtailed their rights in the pursuit of life, liberty, and property to such an extent that their freedom was of little value, while they had lost the protection which they had received from their former owners from motives both of interest and humanity.*
>
> *We repeat, then, in the light of this recapitulation of events, almost too recent to be called history, but which are familiar to us all; and on the most casual examination of the language of these amendments, no one can fail to be impressed with the one pervading purpose found in them all, lying at the foundation of each, and without which none of them would have been even suggested;* **WE MEAN THE FREEDOM OF THE SLAVE RACE**, *the security and firm establishment of that freedom, and the protection of the newly made freeman and citizen from the oppressions of those who had formerly exercised unlimited dominion over him.*

*The 1st section of the 14th article, to which our attention is more specially invited, opens with a definition of citizenship – not only citizenship of the United States, but citizenship of the states. No such definition was previously found in the Constitution, nor had any attempt been made to define it by act of Congress. It had been the occasion of much discussion in the courts, by the executive departments and in the public journals. It had been said by eminent judges that no man was a citizen of the United States except as he was a citizen of one of the states composing the Union. Those, therefore, who had been born and resided always in the District of Columbia, or in the territories, though within the United States, were not citizens. Whether this proposition was sound or not had never been judicially decided. But it had been held by this court, in the celebrated Dred Scott Case, only a few years before the outbreak of the Civil War, that a man of African descent, whether a slave or not, was not and could not be a citizen of a state or of the United States. This decision, while it met the condemnation of some of the ablest statesmen and constitutional lawyers of the country, had never been overruled; and, **if it was to be accepted as a constitutional limitation of the right of citizenship, then all the Negro race who had recently been made freemen were still, not only not citizens, but were incapable of becoming so by anything short of an amendment to the Constitution.***

To remove this difficulty primarily, and to establish a clear and comprehensive definition of citizenship which should declare what should constitute citizenship of the United States and also citizenship of a state, the 1st clause of the 1st section was framed:

> "All persons born or naturalized in the United States and subject to the jurisdiction thereof, are citizens of the United States and of the state wherein they reside."

The first observation we have to make on this clause is that it put at rest both the question which we stated to have been the subject of differences of opinion. It declares that persons may be citizens of the United States without regard to their citizenship of a particular state, and it overturns the Dred Scott decision by making all persons born within the United States and subject to its jurisdiction citizens of the United States. That its main purpose was to establish the citizenship of the Negro can admit of no doubt. . . .

The next observation is more important.

> . . . *It is that the distinction between citizenship of the United States and citizenship of a state is clearly recognized and established.* <u>Not only may a man be a citizen of the United States without being a citizen of a state, but an important element is necessary to convert the former into the latter.</u> **<u>He must reside within the state to make him a citizen of it.</u>** . . .

> *It is quite clear then, that there is a citizenship of the United States and a citizenship of a state, which are distinct from each other and which depend upon different characteristics or circumstances in the individual. . . . [Your legal personality is made up of "rights and duties."]*

Of the privileges and immunities of the citizens of the United States, and of the privileges and immunities of the citizen of the state . . . **it is only the former which are placed by this clause under the protection of the Federal Constitution, and that the latter, whatever they may be, are not intended to have any additional protection by this paragraph of the Amendment** *. . . the latter must rest for their security and protection where they have heretofore rested; for they are not embraced by this paragraph of the Amendment.*

But with the exception of these and a few other restrictions, the entire domain of the privileges and immunities of citizens of the states, as above defined, lay within the constitutional and legislative power of the states, and without that of the Federal government.

Having shown that the privileges and immunities relied on in the argument are those which belong to citizens of the states as such, <u>***and that they are left to the state governments for security and protection and not by this article placed under the special care of the Federal government***</u>*.*

But it is useless to pursue this branch of the inquiry, since we are of opinion that the rights claimed by these plaintiffs in error, if they have any existence, **are not privileges and immunities of citizens of the United States within the meaning of the clause of the 14th Amendment under consideration. This is the fundamental idea upon which our institutions rest, and unless adhered to in the legislation of the country our government will be a Republic only in name.** *- The Slaughter-House Cases*, 83 US 36, 70, 72-74, 78, 80, 110 (1873) (Emphases added).

Nevertheless, most of today's legal scholars simply dismiss *Slaughter-House*. Harvard law professor Laurence Tribe, a liberal icon, writes that "the *Slaughter- House* Cases incorrectly gutted the Privileges or Immunities Clause."[2] Yale law professor Akhil Amar agrees: *"Virtually no serious modern scholar—left, right, and center—thinks that [Slaughter-House] is a plausible reading of the [Fourteenth] Amendment."*[3]

So, why is it that, in this case, the highest court in the Land can make a very clear distinction between a citizen of the United States and a citizen of a state, yet not a single judge, lawyer, senator, member of Congress or the Executive appears to recognize this distinction today? If the Supreme Court has determined that the first sentence of the Fourteenth Amendment was intended primarily to grant national and state citizenship to the four million Freedmen so recently liberated from their former owners, that should be the end of the debate, shouldn't it? After all, the Supreme Court tells us that it is the final arbiter of the Constitution. Former Chief Justice of the U.S. Supreme Court, Charles Evans Hughes, while he was still Governor of New York, stated it this way:

> *"We are under a Constitution, but the Constitution is what the judges say it is, and the judiciary is the safeguard of our liberty and of our property under the Constitution."* - CHARLES EVANS HUGHES, speech before the Chamber of Commerce, Elmira, New York, May 3, 1907.—*Addresses and Papers of Charles Evans Hughes, Governor of New York, 1906–1908*, p. 139 (1908).

Now, the question arises: If the Constitution is what the judges say it is, and if the final 'say' is left to the judges (justices) on the U.S. Supreme Court, how do you explain their ruling that the programs of the New Deal in the 1930s were unconstitutional, and then after a couple of years switching to declare the very opposite for essentially the same programs? Here's how Wikipedia explains "the switch in time that saved nine":

> *"The switch in time that saved nine" is the name given to what was perceived as the sudden jurisprudential shift by Associate Justice Owen J. Roberts of the U.S. Supreme Court in <u>West Coast Hotel Co. v. Parrish</u>, 300 U.S. 379 (1937).*
>
> *Conventional historical accounts portrayed the Court's majority opinion as a strategic **political move** [my bold] to protect the Court's integrity and independence from President Franklin Roosevelt's court- reform bill (also known as the "court- packing plan"), which would have expanded the size of the bench up to 15 justices. The term itself is a reference to the aphorism "A stitch in time saves nine," meaning that preventive maintenance is preferable. - The New Dictionary of Cultural Literacy*, Third Edition.

For more details on the court-packing plan, see Judicial Procedures Reform Bill of 1937. [I'll say there was some real 'preventive maintenance' going on in the Court, would you agree? Just trying to save their skins, eh!]

Through the 1935-36 terms, Roberts had been the deciding vote in several 5-4 decisions invalidating New Deal legislation, casting his vote with the "conservative" bloc of the bench, the so-called "Four Horsemen".[4] This "conservative" wing of the bench is viewed to have been in opposition to the "liberal Three Musketeers".[5] Justice Roberts and Chief Justice Charles Evans Hughes, the remaining two justices, were the center swing votes.[6] The "switch" came in the case *West Coast Hotel Co. v. Parrish*. Roberts joined Chief Justice Hughes and Justices Louis Brandeis, Benjamin N. Cardozo, and Harlan Fiske Stone in upholding a case involving the State of Washington minimum wage law.

The decision was handed down less than two months after President Franklin Delano Roosevelt announced his court- reform bill. Conventional history has painted Roberts's vote as a strategic, politically motivated shift to defeat Roosevelt's proposed legislation, but the historical record lends weight to assertions that Roberts's decision happened much earlier.[7]

Here, then, we come face-to-face with the very problem that our Founders confronted when drafting our Constitution: How do you give a government enough power to administer a constitution without giving it enough power to become despotic, i.e., a government that rules with absolute force? To understand their struggle with this issue, it is necessary to view the world through their eyes. For example, they viewed a constitution as a contract or, in their words, a compact between citizens. Here's how the Constitution for the Commonwealth of Massachusetts[8] states the issue in its Preamble:

> *The end of the institution, maintenance, and administration of government, is to secure the existence of the body politic, to protect it, and to furnish the individuals who compose it with the power of enjoying in safety and tranquility their natural rights, and the blessings of life: and whenever these great objects are not obtained, the people have a right to alter the government, and to take measures necessary for their safety, prosperity and happiness.*

> *The body politic is formed by a voluntary association of individuals: it is a <u>social compact, by which the whole people covenants with each citizen, and each citizen with the whole people</u>, that all shall be governed by certain laws for the common good. It is the duty of the people, therefore, in framing a constitution of government, to provide for an equitable mode of making laws, as well as for an <u>impartial interpretation</u>, and a faithful execution of them; that every man may, at all times, find his security in them.* (Emphases mine.)

In *Rutherford's Institutes of Natural Law,* published in London in 1754, Thomas Rutherford gave an excellent discussion on when a contract reduces one into a condition of servitude and when it does not. I quote it at length, because the principle he sets forth applies with such force to our conditions today.

> *Every compact, in which a man consents to lay himself under an obligation of doing or of avoiding what the law of nature had not otherwise obliged him to do or to avoid, is a diminution of his liberty. Before he had engaged in the compact, he was at liberty either to have done or to have avoided what is contained in the compact. But after he has consented to be thus obliged, he is no longer possessed of the same liberty: he cannot be obliged to do or to avoid what is contained in the compact, and at the same time be at liberty either to do it or to avoid it, as he pleases.*
>
> *But every compact, which implies a diminution of liberty, does not imply likewise a state of subjection. The notion of subjection consists in the obligation of one or more persons to act at the discretion, or according to the judgment and will of others. When,*

> *therefore, the matter of the obligation, which arises from the compact, is so precisely settled from the beginning as to leave nothing to the judgment or will of those to whom we are obliged, the obligation, though it diminishes our liberty, does not place us in a state of subjection. Such a compact gives them a claim upon us, without giving them any authority over us. Their claim is so limited from first to last, by our own act, and according to our own discretion and choice, as never to extend beyond such limitation. This claim, therefore, is all along rather the effect of the power, which we have over ourselves, than the effect of any power which they have over us.* **But when the compact is such from the beginning, as gives them a general demand upon us, and leaves the precise matter of the obligation to be in any respect determined by their discretion and choice, as far as it gives them a right to judge for us, and to prescribe to us, it gives them an authority over us, and places us in a state of subjection to this authority.** - Rutherford's *Institutes of Natural Law*, 2nd American Ed., p. 436 (1832).[9]

The thrust of his explanation is this: When those who are appointed to administer the contract are given discretion to interpret it and, therefore, execute it as they see fit, then the contract amounts to slavery or servitude. On the other hand, when the administrators merely carry out the terms of the contract without discretion to interpret is, then the parties are free, except as limited by the express terms of the contract.

As we have seen in the Massachusetts Constitution, a constitution is a contract or compact among the citizens of the state or nation. Regrettably, the judiciary of our nation has taken it upon itself to 'interpret' the Constitution at its discretion, as it sees fit, i.e., it interprets it in the manner that provides the largest possible aggregation of power or jurisdiction for the Federal Government, the very government that employs the judiciary. This is not simply a recent trend. Read the words of Thomas Jefferson on this same subject:

> *The judiciary of the United States is the subtle corps of sappers and miners constantly working under ground to undermine the foundations of our confederated fabric. They are construing our constitution from a co-ordination of a general and special government to a general and supreme one alone.*
>
> *This will lay all things at their feet, and they are too well versed in English law to forget the maxim, "<u>boni judicis est ampliare jurisdictionem</u>."* [It is the part of a good judge to enlarge jurisdiction.] - Thomas Jefferson, letter to Thomas Ritchie, December 25, 1820. *The Writings of Thomas Jefferson*, ed. Paul L. Ford, vol. 10, pp. 170-71. A similar statement is made in Jefferson's Autobiography, *Writings*, vol. 1, pp. 112-13.

That is precisely what the Supreme Court did in the 1930s, when it reversed itself and upheld Roosevelt's "New Deal" legislation, namely, it enlarged the jurisdiction of the Federal Government to include virtually every aspect of our lives. One of the benefits of such expansion of federal jurisdiction is that it gives more power, perks and emoluments to the federal judiciary, a conflict of interest and a violation of their oaths to do impartial justice. Their oath is set forth at 28 U.S.C. § 453. *Oaths of justices and judges.*

Each justice or judge of the United States shall take the following oath or affirmation before performing the duties of his office:

> "*I, XXX XXX, do solemnly swear (or affirm) that I will administer justice without respect to persons, and do equal right to the poor and to the rich, and that I will faithfully and **impartially** discharge and perform all the duties incumbent upon me as XXX under the Constitution and laws of the United States. So help me God.*" (My emphasis)

This conflict-of-interest means that the Federal Government, through its judiciary, sits in judgment upon itself. Yet, didn't the Massachusetts Constitution call for '*impartial interpretation*'? How can you expect to receive impartial justice from courts which are presided over by judges employed by the very government that you are challenging and by whom these same judges are employed?

The courts are sometimes referred to as "lions under the throne" of the British Constitution. This expresses how eager the judiciary is to claw at government if its actions hinder individuals' rights and liberties. It is essential in a free society that the judges be and appear to be independent of the executive and legislative branches of government in order to garner public confidence in their decisions.

Proverbs 22:28 says, "*Remove not the ancient landmark, which thy fathers have set.*" What is "the ancient landmark, which thy fathers have set"? In ancient times, property was defined by the setting of stone pillars at the limits of the land. To remove these landmarks was considered a serious offense. Hence, landmarks define our inheritance. The landmark, which our Fathers have set for us, our inheritance, is the Constitution and the stone pillars within it by which we measure the extent of our freedoms.

Thus, when our rights and duties under the Constitution are so precisely settled from the beginning as to leave nothing to the judgment or will of those to whom we are obliged, they become our constitutional landmarks and, though they diminish our liberty, do not place us in a state of subjection. However, when those constitutional landmarks, those stone pillars are no longer set in stone but are interpreted to be moveable at the will or discretion of judges, then the Constitution, as newly interpreted, gives the Federal Government a general demand upon us, and leaves the precise matter of our obligation to it to be determined by the discretion and choice of those judges. Theses judges, these "lions under the throne," now possess a right to judge for us, to prescribe to us, and have arrogated unto themselves an authority over us that effectively places us in a state of subjection to the authority of the Federal Government. We no longer have the rule of law – and our law is the Constitution[10] – but the rule of men and women, sitting on the judicial bench.

In short, when an agreement, compact or constitution gives to those who administer it the right, power or jurisdiction to interpret it at their will, whim or discretion, that document places one into a state of subjection to those who administer it. Let us now see how this principle played out in our next case study.

~ *United States v. Wong Kim Ark* ~
United States v Wong Kim Ark, U.S. 649 (1898), is perhaps the most definitive case in the entire history of the Supreme Court dealing with the issues of citizenship and other political and civil rights questions. It was a U. S. Supreme Court decision that set an important legal precedent about the role of *jus soli* (birth in the

United States) as a factor in determining a person's claim to United States citizenship. The citizenship status of Wong (a man born in the United States to Chinese parents around 1870) was challenged[11] because of a law restricting Chinese immigration and prohibiting immigrants from China from becoming naturalized U.S. citizens,[12] but the Supreme Court ruled that the citizenship language in the Fourteenth Amendment to the Constitution could not be limited in its effect by an act of Congress.[13]

The debate surrounding the *Wong Kim Ark* case highlighted disagreements over the precise meaning of the phrase "subject to the jurisdiction thereof" in the Fourteenth Amendment's Citizenship Clause.

The 14th Amendment's citizenship clause, according to the court's majority, had to be interpreted in light of English common law,[14] which had included all native- born children except for those who were: (1) born to foreign rulers or diplomats, (2) born on foreign public ships, or (3) born to enemy forces engaged in hostile occupation of the country's territory.[15] The majority held that the "subject to the jurisdiction" phrase in the 14th Amendment specifically incorporated these exceptions (plus a fourth – namely, that Indian tribes "not taxed" were not considered subject to U.S. jurisdiction[16])—and that since none of these exceptions applied to Wong's situation, Wong was a U.S. citizen, regardless of the fact that his parents were not U.S. citizens (and were, in fact, ineligible ever to become U.S. citizens because of the Chinese Exclusion Act).

~ **Dissent** ~
Chief Justice Melville Fuller was joined by Justice John Harlan in a dissenting opinion which, in the words of one analyst, was "elaborately drawn and, for the most part, may be said to be

predicated upon the recognition of the international law doctrine".[17] Fuller argued that the history of U.S. citizenship law had broken with English common law tradition after independence—citing as an example the embracing in the U.S. of the right of expatriation (giving up of one's native citizenship) and the rejection of the contrary British doctrine of perpetual allegiance.[18] The minority argued that the principle of *jus sanguinis* (that is, the concept of a child inheriting his or her father's citizenship by descent regardless of birthplace) had been more pervasive in U.S. legal history since independence.[19]

Pointing to the language of the Civil Rights Act of 1866, which declared to be citizens "all persons born in the United States and not subject to any foreign power, excluding Indians not taxed", and which was enacted into law only two months before the 14th Amendment was proposed by Congress, the minority argued that "it is not open to reasonable doubt that the words 'subject to the jurisdiction thereof,' in the amendment, were used as synonymous with the words 'and not subject to any foreign power'".[20] In the view of the minority, excessive reliance on *jus soli* (birthplace) as the principal determiner of citizenship would lead to an untenable state of affairs in which "the children of foreigners, happening to be born to them while passing through the country, whether of royal parentage or not, or whether of the Mongolian, Malay or other race, were eligible to the presidency, while children of our citizens, born abroad, were not".[21]

~ SYLLABUS ~

The following are headnotes from the Syllabus: (9) Before the Civil Rights Act, April 9, 1866, c. 31, Sec. 1 (14 Stat. 27), or the fourteenth amendment to the constitution, all white persons born within the sovereignty of the United States, whether children of citizens or of foreigners, excepting only children of ambassadors or public ministers of a foreign government, were natural-born citizens of the United States.

(10) The refusal of congress to permit the naturalization of Chinese persons cannot exclude Chinese persons born in this country from the operation of the constitutional declaration that all persons born in the United States, and subject to the jurisdiction thereof, are citizens of the United States.

(11) Chinese persons born out of the United States, remaining subjects, of the emperor of China, and not having become citizens of the United States, are entitled to the protection of and owe allegiance to the United States so long as they are <u>permitted by the United States to reside here</u>, and are "subject to the jurisdiction thereof" in the same sense as all other aliens residing in the United States, and their children "born in the United States" cannot be less "subject to the jurisdiction thereof."

(12) A child born in the United States, of parents of Chinese descent, who, at the time of his birth, are subjects of the emperor of China, but have a permanent domicile and residence in the United States, and are there carrying on business, and are not employed in any diplomatic or official capacity under the emperor of China, becomes, at the time of his birth, a citizen of the United States.

~ ANALYSIS ~

This analysis comes from my Mentor, John Benson, author of, *Taxation by Misrepresentation, The Truth about Taxes in Plain English*, and which I recommend to you as strongly as I can. (http://www.no1040tax.com)

John started out by explaining that there was a very strong political undercurrent in this case but which is never mentioned in the case itself. Here's the background that must be understood before you can really make sense of this decision.

> Program Two: *"Between Two Worlds"* The 1882 Exclusion Act prohibited Chinese laborers from entering the country and becoming citizens. It also ushered in the most violent decade in Chinese-American history, with assault, arson and murder becoming ever-present dangers for a people marginalized in the eyes of the law.
>
> Part Two of **BECOMING AMERICAN: The Chinese Experience** *tells the story of these hostile years when Chinese Americans existed in a kind of limbo, denied the rights of their new country and no longer at home in their former one. They found refuge in Chinatowns, insular worlds that provided a sense of security and the companionship of kinsmen. But as few Chinese women were able to immigrate due to both Chinese custom and U.S. law, the majority of Chinese men could not establish families here. As age, disease and death claimed the earlier immigrants, the number of Chinese declined dramatically almost to the point of vanishing from American life.*

> But those here clung to American life and values, and fought for their rights using the only tools of democracy available to them: the courts. Recognizing that the Constitution offered protection to all people in America, not merely its citizens, the Chinese boldly filed over 10,000 lawsuits challenging laws and practices designed to harass and oppress them. When Wong Kim Ark, a 22-year-old cook born in San Francisco, sued to be considered a citizen, it was a decisive victory against discriminatory legislation. Moyers says, "It took the Supreme Court to remind the government that the words of the 14th Amendment meant just what they said. A person born in America was American." - **A Bill Moyers Special** – *Becoming an American: The Chinese Experience* (accessed 9/1/2011 http://www.pbs.org/becomingamerican/ap_prog2.html)

John pointed out that the Chinese, just as the black slaves, had suffered grievously in their respective states because neither those states nor the Federal Government would give them the protections secured to "all persons," not just citizens, by the 14th Amendment. Faced with a politically untenable situation in the Country, mob violence, and the like, the Supreme Court felt it had to step into the breach and put out the fires raging in the Country. The Warren Court did the same thing in 1954 when it ruled that the separate-but-equal doctrine[22] was unconstitutional.

Regrettably, as John taught us, the Court failed to follow what had been the consistent rulings of the Supreme Court itself over the life of the Country since the Constitution was ratified. Here are some of those prior Supreme Court decisions.

In *The Venus*, 12 U.S. 253 (1814), Justice Henry Brockholst Livingston, who was a Lieutenant Colonel in the New York Line and an aide-de-camp to General Benedict Arnold, before the latter's defection to the British, writing for a unanimous Court, quoted from *The Law of Nations*, by Emmerich de Vattel,[23] in the following passage:

> *Vattel, who, though not very full to this point, is more explicit and more satisfactory on it than any other whose work has fallen into my hands, says*
>
> *The citizens are the members of the civil society; bound to this society by certain duties, and subject to its authority, they equally participate in its advantages. The natives or indigenes are those born in the country of parents who are citizens. Society not being able to subsist and to perpetuate itself but by the children of the citizens, those children naturally follow the condition of their fathers, and succeed to all their rights.*
>
> *The inhabitants, as distinguished from citizens, are strangers who are permitted to settle and stay in the country. Bound by their residence to the society, they are subject to the laws of the state while they reside there, and they are obliged to defend it because it grants them protection, though they do not participate in all the rights of citizens. They enjoy only the advantages which the laws or custom gives them. The perpetual inhabitants are those who have received the right of perpetual residence. These are a kind of citizens of an inferior order, and are united and subject to the society, without participating in all its advantages. - Id.* at 289-290 (quoting *Vattel*, Book I, Chapter 19, § 212, of the English translation of

1797 (p. 110) (retrieved on September 3, 2011 on http://books.google.com/books?id=z8b8rrzRc7AC&dq=E

This very same passage is quoted by Chief Justice Fuller, in his dissent, at page 708 of *Wong Kim Ark*. C.J. Fuller then explains:

> "The true bond which connects the child with the body politic is not the matter of an inanimate piece of land, but the moral relations of his parentage. . . . The place of birth produces no change in the rule that **children follow the condition of their fathers, for it is not naturally the place of birth that gives rights, but extraction.**" (quoting, in part, from *Vattel* at § 216) (my emphasis).

In *Shanks v. DuPont*, 28 U.S. 242, 245 (1830), Justice Story, writing for the Court, stated:

> "If she was not of age, then she might well be deemed under the circumstances of this for **children born in a country, continuing while under age in the family of the father, partake of his national character as a citizen of that country.**" (my emphasis).

The next case is *Minor v. Happersett*, 88 U.S. 162 (1874). Chief Justice Waite delivered the opinion of the Court, including this passage:

> "Whoever, then, was one of the people of either of these States when the Constitution of the United States was adopted, became ipso facto a citizen – a member of the nation created by its adoption. He was one of the persons associating together to form the

nation, and was, consequently, one of its original citizens. As to this there has never been a doubt. Disputes have arisen as to whether or not certain persons or certain classes of persons were part of the people at the time, but never as to their citizenship if they were.

Additions might always be made to the citizenship of the United States in two ways: first, by birth, and second, by naturalization. This is apparent from the Constitution itself, for it provides that 'no person except a natural-born citizen, or a citizen of the United States at the time of the adoption of the Constitution, shall be eligible to the office of President,' and that Congress shall have power 'to establish a uniform rule of naturalization.' Thus new created by naturalization.

The Constitution does not, in words, say who shall be natural-born citizens. Resort must be had elsewhere to ascertain that. **At common-law, with the nomenclature of which the framers of the Constitution were familiar, it was never doubted that all children born in a country of parents who were its citizens became themselves, upon their birth, citizens also.** *These were natives, or natural-born citizens, as distinguished from aliens or foreigners. Some authorities go further and include as citizens children born within the jurisdiction without reference to the citizenship of their parents. As to this class there have been doubts, but never as to the first. For the purposes of this case it is not necessary to solve these doubts. It is sufficient for everything we have now to consider that all children born of citizen parents within the jurisdiction are themselves citizens." - Id.* at 167-68 (footnote omitted) (my emphasis).

It is apparent from these passages that children born of those who were citizens were themselves citizens by virtue of their parents' citizenship; they did not require the 14th Amendment in order to partake of such citizenship.

Justice Gray, writing for the majority in *Wonk Kim Ark*, quotes with approval this part of the *Happersett* case in *Wong Kim Ark*, 169 U.S. at 679-80.

However, if the *Wong Kim Ark* majority were to have abided by the understanding that the citizenship of children followed their parents' citizenship, the political firestorm ablaze in the Nation at that time would not have been quelled. Wong Kim Ark would not have been recognized as a citizen, nor would the other tens of thousands of Chinese who were frustrated by their lack of citizenship. The majority faced some hard choices. Perhaps Justice Oliver Wendell Holmes, Jr., stated the principle best suited to the *Wong Kim Ark* majority decision, although in a different context:

> "Great cases, like hard cases, make bad law. For great cases are called great not by reason of their real importance in shaping the law of the future, but because of some accident of immediate overwhelming interest which appeals to the feelings and distorts the judgment. These immediate interests exercise a kind of hydraulic pressure which makes what previously was clear seem doubtful, and before which even well settled principles of law will bend."
> - Northern Securities Co. v. United States, 193 U.S. 197, 400-401 (1904) (Holmes, J., dissenting).

The Supreme Court justices who signed onto the majority decision in *Wong Kim Ark* faced a very difficult national crisis not of their own making but which had been caused by the very same problem that had faced the Founders in drafting the Constitution: How do you unite a Nation divided along racial lines?

Even today, our laws are not free of racial overtones. Read 42 U.S.C. § 1981:

> *(a) Statement of equal rights*
> **All persons within the jurisdiction of the United States** *shall have the same right in every State and Territory to make and enforce contracts, to sue, be parties, give evidence, and to the full and equal benefit of all laws and proceedings for the security of persons and property as is enjoyed by* **white citizens**, *and shall be subject to like punishment, pains, penalties, taxes, licenses, and exactions of every kind, and to no other.* (My emphasis)

Our Nation is not unique in attempting to resolve this problem peaceably. The same problem that faced our Founders in drafting the Constitution has plagued other nations the world over: Britain in Ireland, South Africa with Apartheid, Iraq and the Kurds, Mexico and its native Indian groups, and I'm sure you could think of others.

For good or ill, these problems have been laid at the steps of the Supreme Court to resolve. So, in 1898, when the Chinese discrimination suits by the thousands clogged the Nation's courts, the Supreme Court felt it had to step into the breach, as I mentioned, and resolve the problem that the Executive and Legislative branches of our national government had not been able to resolve, indeed, a problem which those branches had exacerbated. I don't mean to paint the Supreme Court as the great savior and healer of the Nation, for the problem had been made much worse by its dreadful decision in *Dred Scott v. Sandford*.

Facts of the Case:
Dred Scott was a slave of African descent who had lived in Illinois (a free state) and in a part of the Louisiana Territory, where slavery was outlawed by the Missouri Compromise of 1820. Scott sued his owner in federal court. Sandford, his owner, claimed that an African slave could not sue as a citizen of the United States under Article III of the Constitution.

Question Presented to the Court:
Was Dred Scott a citizen of the United States?

Decision:
Chief Justice Taney, writing for the 7-2 majority, held that Dred Scott was not a citizen of the United States under Articles III & IV of the Constitution, that he could not sue in federal court under Article III, and that the court below did not have jurisdiction to hear Dred Scott's lawsuit.

The most reasonable and sensible opinion in this dreadful case was written by Justice Curtis and is well worth reading. Had the majority simply ruled that the Declaration of Independence had set the foundation for the equality of all men,[24] we would not now be faced with the problem of two classes of citizenship in the United States.

Consequently, just as the hard case of *Dred Scott* made necessary the bad law of citizenship in the 14th Amendment, so, also, it made necessary the even worse law of *Wong Kim Ark*, wherein, not just those of African or Chinese descent were brought under the feudal-law jurisdiction of the great Federal Manor, but all persons of whatever race were made to bear the yoke of feudal allegiance. Here's how Chief Justice Fuller described the majority's citizenship rule in *Wong Kim Ark*:

"The rule was the outcome of the connection in feudalism between the individual and the soil on which he lived, and the allegiance due was that of liegemen to their liege lord. It was not local and temporary, as was the obedience to the laws owed by aliens within the dominions of the Crown, but permanent and indissoluble, and not to be cancelled by any change of time or place or circumstances.

And it is this rule, pure and simple, which it is asserted determined citizenship of the United States during the entire period prior to the passage of the act of April 9, 1866, and the ratification of the Fourteenth Amendment, and governed the meaning of the words "citizen of the United States" and "natural-born citizen" used in the Constitution as originally framed and adopted. I submit that no such rule obtained during the period referred to, and that those words bore no such construction; that the act of April 9, 1866, expressed the contrary rule; that the Fourteenth Amendment prescribed the same rule as the act, and that, if that amendment bears the construction now put upon it, **it imposed the English common law rule on this country for the first time, and made it "absolute and unbending" just as Great Britain was being relieved from its inconveniences."* - Wong Kim Ark*, 169 U.S. at 707 (Fuller, J., dissenting) (describing the citizenship rule adopted by the majority) (emphasis mine).

~ *WONG KIM ARK* WAS A POLITICAL DECISION ~

So, as you can plainly see, the *Wong Kim Ark* majority did exactly what the *Dred Scott* majority did: they issued a political decision, not a decision based upon the fundamental laws and principles upon which our Nation was formed. Today, you and I, my readers, are now struggling to get out from under the downstream effects of these decisions.

John has now completed his book on taxes, to be followed by a book on the rights and duties of the jury. His belief is that the political leaders and judges of our day are no better and no worse than those of yesteryear and that they will not address the issues, which I raise here.

Glenn and John raised these same issues in the seminars they taught across the United States. Because they raised these issues, they were unjustly prosecuted and imprisoned. John and Glenn have now come to believe, and I agree with them, that the only means by which to address these issues are the means employed by our people in the past, namely, through educated members of our juries.

To effect real change in this Country, you need to have the support of a sizable mass of people; one or even a few people cannot effect change. When, as now, the politicians and the courts have seemed impotent or simply unwilling to administer the affairs of the people in a manner suited to their rights and immunities, the American juries have stepped up to the plate, so to speak, and have simply refused to enforce what they considered to be unjust laws.

Perhaps the most famous such case was that of John Peter Zenger, charged with printing seditious libels of the Governor of the Colony of New York, William Cosby in 1735. Despite the fact that the jury was aware that Zenger had printed the alleged libels (the only issue the court said the jury was free to decide, as the court deemed the truth or falsity of the statements to be irrelevant), nevertheless, the jury returned a verdict of "Not Guilty."

Juries refused to enforce the Alien and Sedition Acts, in the early 1800s, the Fugitive Slave Acts, in the middle of the 19th Century, and again refused to enforce the Prohibition laws in the 1930s. So, the Constitution, itself, has a built-in circuit-breaker, if you will, a means to stop the harm of destructive acts and runaway laws of government when, in the People's conscience, such acts and laws are either unjust, immoral or simply not in keeping with the principles of our Republican form of government.

The duty of the juries to act as a sort of "super-governing" check on the other three Branches of government has been exercised only sparingly by the People. However, there can be no doubt that this duty does, indeed, exist and that it was part of the purposes of the jury clauses in the Constitution and in the Bill of Rights. Let us, once again, turn to the Declaration of Independence:

> *We hold these truths to be self-evident: That all men are created equal; that they are endowed by their Creator with certain unalienable rights; that among these are life, liberty, and the pursuit of happiness; that, to secure these rights, governments are instituted among men, deriving their just powers from the consent of the governed; that whenever any form of government becomes destructive of these ends,* **it is the right of the people to alter** *or to abolish* **it**, *and to institute new government, laying its foundation on such principles, and organizing its powers in such form, as to them shall seem most likely to effect their safety and happiness. .*
>
> *. . But when a long train of abuses and usurpations, pursuing invariably the same Object evinces a design to reduce them under absolute Despotism,* **it is their right, it is their duty, to throw off such Government, and to provide new Guards for their future security***.* (Emphasis mine).

As the authors of the Declaration admonished,

> *Prudence, indeed, will dictate that Governments long established should not be changed for light and transient causes; and accordingly all experience hath shewn that mankind are more disposed to suffer, while evils are sufferable than to right themselves by abolishing the forms to which they are accustomed.*

It is my profound belief that many Americans will, when educated as to the "long train of abuses and usurpations" that have taken place, always "pursuing invariably the same Object" and that "evinces a design to reduce them under absolute Despotism," will rise to their duty and, if shown how, will once more bring their government back under control.

Look at the states where the voters have passed medical marijuana and right-to-die laws.[25] Yet, the Federal Government arrogates to itself the supposed right to ignore and counteract such laws, to ignore the will of the people of those states. The sole constitutional authority for the Federal Government to make laws regulating the health laws of those states comes from the 14th Amendment.

Sadly, the original Constitution of limited and enumerated powers did not survive the Civil War or the War Between the States.

Instead, the Country is now ruled under the 14th Amendment, and even then, only as nine justices sitting on the Supreme Court see fit. Today, we have Government by Judiciary.

In his great work, *Government by Judiciary, The Transformation of the Fourteenth Amendment,* Harvard constitutional scholar, Raoul Berger, states in the first sentence of his book,

> *"The Fourteenth Amendment is the case study par excellence of what Justice Harlan described as the Supreme Court's "exercise of the amending power," its continuing revision of the Constitution under the guise of interpretation."* - **Raoul Berger**, *Government by Judiciary: The Transformation of the Fourteenth Amendment,* Foreword by Forrest McDonald (2nd ed.) (Indianapolis: Liberty Fund, 1997). Chapter: 1: Introduction
>
> Accessed from http://oll.libertyfund.org/title/675/106892/2250519 on 2011-09-05 (quoting *Reynolds v. Sims*, 377 U.S. 533, 591 (1964)).

Professor Berger argues forcefully, supported by massive evidence, that the Court has virtually subverted the Constitution, by handing down rulings that are nothing short of their own personal predilections.

I urge you to read this wonderful book, free online at http://oll.libertyfund.org/index.php?option=com_staticxt&staticfile=show.php&title=675.

Here is a brief summary of the thesis of this great work: "

> *It is the thesis of this book that the Supreme Court is not empowered to rewrite the Constitution, that in its transformation of the Fourteenth Amendment it has demonstrably done so. Thereby the Justices, who are virtually unaccountable, irremovable, and irreversible, have taken over from the people control of their own destiny, an awesome exercise of power. When Chief Justice Marshall stated that the function of the legislature is to make the law, that of the*

judiciary to interpret it,[26] he echoed Francis Bacon's admonition two hundred years earlier.[27] Much less are judges authorized to revise the Constitution, for as Justice Black, deriding the notion that the Court was meant to keep the Constitution "in tune with the times," stated, "The Constitution makers knew the need for change and provided for it" by the amendment process of Article V,[28] whereby the people reserved unto themselves the right to change the Constitution. Having created a prepotent Congress, being well aware of the greedy expansiveness of power, and knowing that power can be malign as well as benign, the Founders designed the judiciary to keep Congress within its prescribed bounds,[29] what James Bradley Thayer and Learned Hand later called "policing" the constitutional boundaries.[30] Within those boundaries, stated Justice James Iredell, one of the ablest of the Founders, the legislature was to be free of judicial interference."[31] Berger, supra, Chapter: appendix b: *Judicial Administration of Local Matters*

- Accessed from http://oll.libertyfund.org/title/675/106989/22 50542 on 2011-09-05. (The footnotes within this paragraph are Professor Berger's.)

As you can see, we are not alone, we are not simply a fringe group, baying at the moon, complaining about all the injustices perpetrated by those who sit in the seats of power, whether in Congress, the Executive Branch of Government or on the judicial bench. The Supreme Court's interpretation of the 14th Amendment has effectively replaced the Constitution of 1789 with Government by Judiciary, where the Federal Government is Lord and Master, and the states are little more than field operating units of the government in Washington, D.C.

Now that we've taken a look at how the *Wong Kim Ark* majority issued what was essentially a political, rather than a legal, decision, let's take a look at what the legal analysis should have considered.

WONG KIM ARK IGNORED THE NATURE OF OUR REVOLUTION!

The first, and most fundamental, question to ask about *Wong Kim Ark* is this: Can a free people govern themselves, or is it necessary that they have a superior or sovereign over them in order to have a viable government? In other words, is it necessary that there be two classes of persons in a society – sovereign(s) and subjects – in order for government to exist?

This may sound like a foolish question, but the great English jurist, Sir William Blackstone, whom the courts of this Land quote so often and with such reverence, maintained that society required that there be a superior over the people in order to have viable government. Blackstone explained that the king "is, and ought to be absolute; that is, so far absolute that there is no legal authority that can either delay or resist him" *Commentaries on the Laws of England* (1765–1769) (vol. 2, pp. 238–250).

> *"Is self-government possible? Or must there be a sovereign? Can limitations be set upon all power? Or is the notion of a superior to command, essential to the idea of municipal law?* **According to the English doctrine, as stated by Blackstone, it was essential to the idea of law, that there must be a superior, that is, they [our Founders] were face to**

face with his, Blackstone's, definition of law. That "law is a rule of action prescribed by the supreme power in a state."[32] This position, says Judge Wilson,[33] *is only a branch of a more extended principle upon which a* **plan of systematic despotism** *has lately been formed in England.* **The principle is, that all human laws must be prescribed by a superior.** *This principle I mean not now to examine; suffice to say, that another principle, very different in its nature and operations, forms the basis of sound jurisprudence. Laws derived from the pure source of equality and justice must be founded on the consent of those whose obedience they require:"* Chisholm v. Georgia, 2 Dall. [U.S.] 419 (1793).

"The idea of sovereignty, which obtained at the time of the Revolution, regarded as the essential attributes of sovereignty, inequality and unlimited power. Inequality and personal superiority were repudiated by the Declaration of Independence. What was substituted in its stead? Certainly, so far as this question is concerned, they acted upon an entirely different principle. I may add, upon one never before practiced in any country, viz.: The one just mentioned, that power is never to be exercised as of personal right. The doctrine of representation was not of recent origin: **the doctrine of consent was at the basis of English law, although Blackstone seems to have omitted to notice the decisions of the judges of England upon those questions:"** *Middleton v. Cross,* 2 Atkyns, 65; *Matthews v. Burdette,* 2 Salk. 672. - **James DeWitt Andrews,** *The Works of James Wilson* 569 (Vol. II, 1896)[34] (my emphasis; bracketed words are mine).

Regrettably, as the *Wong Kim Ark* majority decision so aptly demonstrates, the idea of sovereignty vested in the Federal Government has haunted our judiciary like a ghost. In 1856, the Court stated, "the government itself, which gave the command, cannot be sued without its own consent." *Murray's Lessee v. Hoboken Land & Improvement Co.*, 59 U.S. 272, 283 (1856).[35] In substance and effect, what the Court was communicating was this: just as the King of England, the only Sovereign in that country, could not be sued by his subjects without his permission, so also the Federal Government, sitting as the Sovereign in this Country, could not be sued by its subjects, the citizens of this Country, without its consent. This is the origin, as far as I can determine, of the judicially-created doctrine of the Government's claim of "sovereign immunity, i.e., that it may not be sued unless it has consented to such suit.

In his course manual, John included the Kentucky case *Gaines v. Buford*, 31 Ky. (1 Dana) 481 (1833), in which this passage was cited by John as perhaps the best he'd ever read regarding the idea of sovereignty in government:

> "I shall notice one idea more in defense of the act, and only one. It is the appeal made in the preamble to the <u>sovereign power of the State</u>. I do not admit that there is any <u>sovereign power</u>, in the literal meaning of the terms, to be found anywhere in our system of government. The people possess, as it regards their governments, a <u>revolutionary sovereign power</u>: but so long as the governments remain which they have instituted, to establish justice and "to secure the enjoyment of the rights of life, liberty and property, and of pursuing happiness," <u>sovereign power</u>, or, which I take to be the same thing, power without limitation, is nowhere to be found in any branch or department of the government, either state

or national, nor indeed of all of them put together. The Constitution of the United States expressly forbids the passage of any bill of attainder, or <u>ex post facto</u> law, or the granting of any title of nobility, by the general or the state government. The same instrument likewise limits the powers of the general government to those expressly granted, and places many other restrictions upon the power of state governments. The constitutions of the different States likewise contain many prohibitions and limitations of power. The tenth article of our State constitution, consisting of twenty-eight sections, is made up of restrictions and prohibitions upon legislative and judicial power, and concludes with the emphatic declaration, "that everything in this article is excerpted out of the general powers of government, and shall forever remain inviolate; and that all laws contrary thereto, or contrary to this constitution, shall be void."

These numerous limitations and restrictions prove that the idea of <u>sovereignty in government</u> was not tolerated by the wise founders of our systems. "<u>Sovereign State</u>" are cabalistic words not understood by the disciple of liberty who has been in our constitutional schools. It is an appropriate phrase when applied to an absolute despotism. I firmly believe that the idea of sovereign power in the government of a republic is incompatible with the existence and permanent foundation of civil liberty and the rights of property. The history of man in all ages shown the necessity of the strongest checks upon power, whether it be exercised by one man, a few, or many. Our revolution broke up the foundations of sovereignty in government, and our written constitutions have carefully guarded against

> *the baneful influence of such an idea henceforth and forever. I cannot, therefore, recognize the appeal to the sovereignty of the States as a justification of the act in question."* - *Id.* at 500-501 (**Underwood, J**.) (emphasis by Judge Underwood).

Nevertheless, 65 years later, the ghost of the feudal principle that sovereignty is somehow vested within the Federal Government rears its ugly head, and feudal sovereignty in the government is once again imposed upon this Nation by 7 out of 9 Justices on the High Court in *Wong Kim Ark* in their construction of the Citizenship Clause of the Fourteenth Amendment.

Although not spoken of often in today's political and judicial circles, there are really only two legitimate sources of national lawmaking authority in this Nation: the People and Congress. Here's how Professor Andrews states this idea:

> *"In America, there is recognized two distinct branches of legislative power. The one is exercised by the electors, or voters, as the immediate representatives of the people, and now habitually exercised in elections and assemblages, which have become familiar in the States, under the name of constitutional conventions, because the operations are confined and limited to the enactment of political legislation. Grimpkins Arg. 1 Hill, South Carolina, 16; Jamison Constitutional Convention, 21-22.*
>
> *The other is ordinary legislation exercised by Congress, or the state legislators, chosen by the electors to represent the whole people. The former was unknown in England."* - **Andrews**, supra, at 70.

While sovereignty does not exist in government, state or federal, it does exist within the People themselves, those who established, ordained and ratified the Constitution.

In the words of Justice James Wilson, "sovereignty is and remains in the people." Jamison's *Constitutional Convention*, p. 20. Here's how Benjamin Franklin expressed the principle:

> "In free Governments the rulers are the servants, and the people their superiors & sovereigns." - **Benjamin Franklin**, *Remarks in Framing Convention*, 1787 as summarized by Madison in his record (Emphasis per original).

Here's how the first Chief Justice of the Supreme Court for the United States stated the principle that sovereignty resides in the People:

> "It will be sufficient to observe briefly that the **sovereignties** in Europe, and particularly in England, **exist on feudal principles**. That system considers the Prince as the sovereign, and the people as his subjects; it regards his person as the object of allegiance, and excludes the idea of his being on an equal footing with a subject, either in a court of justice or elsewhere. That system contemplates him as being the fountain of honor and authority, and from his grace and grant derives all franchises, immunities and privileges; it is easy to perceive that such a sovereign could not be amenable to a court of justice, or subjected to judicial controul and actual constraint. It was of necessity, therefore, that suability became incompatible with such sovereignty. Besides, the Prince having all the Executive powers, the judgment of the courts would, in fact, be only

> *monitory, not mandatory to him, and a capacity to be advised is a distinct thing from a capacity to be sued. The same feudal ideas run through all their jurisprudence, and constantly remind us of the distinction between the Prince and the subject. No such ideas obtain here;* **at the Revolution, the sovereignty devolved on the people, and they are truly the sovereigns of the country**, *but they are sovereigns without subjects (unless the African slaves among us may be so called), and have none to govern but themselves; the citizens of America are equal as fellow citizens, and as joint tenants in the sovereignty." - Chisholm v. Georgia*, 2 U.S. 419, 471-472 (1793) (**Jay, Chief Justice**) (my emphasis).

In *Slaughter-House*, **Justice Bradley**, makes the following statement on this topic:

> *"The Declaration of Independence, which was the first political act of* **the American people in their independent sovereign capacity**, *lays the foundation of our National existence upon this broad proposition,"*

>> *"That all men are created equal; that they are endowed by their Creator with certain inalienable rights; that among these are life, liberty, and the pursuit of happiness."* - 83 U.S. at 116-117 (**Bradley, Justice**, dissenting) (my emphasis).

There can, therefore, be absolutely no doubt that the People have been the sovereigns of this Nation and have been repeatedly recognized as such by the courts of this Land. The question which our Founders faced arises once again, as Justice James Wilson stated it: "*Is self- government possible? Or must there be a sovereign?*"

More to the point, for our purposes, does the term "citizens of the United States," as used in the Fourteenth Amendment, define the "sovereigns" of this Nation or its "subjects."

Justice Gray, writing for the majority in *Wong Kim Ark*, recognized that the People are the sovereigns:

> "*The words "people of the United States" and "citizens" are synonymous terms, and mean the same thing. They both describe the political body who, according to our republican institutions, form the sovereignty, and who hold the power and conduct the government through their representatives. They are what we familiarly call the "**sovereign people**," and **every citizen is one of this people and a constituent member of this sovereignty**.*" - *Wong Kim Ark*, 169 U.S. at 717 (quoting *Dred Scott v. Sandford*, 393 U.S. 393, 404 (1856)

Despite his recognizing the People as sovereigns, Justice Gray compares and contrasts citizens in the United States with the King's subjects in England, throughout his majority opinion. He spends several pages (667-674) in his effort to discard the rule of international law, namely, that citizenship of children followed the citizenship of the father, or the mother, if born out of wedlock.[36] Instead, he adopts the common-law rule of territoriality, namely, where you are born determines your citizenship. This rule, which Chief Justice Fuller excoriates in his dissent,[37] has, as we have seen, caused dreadful downstream consequences with the issue of what the media has dubbed "anchor babies," children born here of aliens, legal and illegal, and used as a pretext for gaining residence and citizenship in the United States, as well as qualifying for state and federal entitlement benefits.

While this, alone, would have been sufficient cause for alarm at his decision, even worse is the fact that, by adopting this feudal, common-law rule, the *Wong Kim Ark* decision provided a legal foundation upon which others built a superstructure, importing and imposing upon "all persons," not just minorities, the balance of the feudal inconveniences: allegiance, subjection, the government's "sovereign immunity, and the like.

Effectively, Justice Gray's *Wong Kim Ark* decision opened the floodgates to the sewage of the feudal law and effectively rent asunder the chains of the Constitution. If "all persons" here were now "completely subject to the political jurisdiction of the United States, owing them direct and immediate allegiance," well . . . it doesn't get much more feudal than that, does it?

Let's take a look at what the very first Congress required in order for an alien to acquire national citizenship. Here's the Act itself (The First Naturalization Law of March 26, 1790 (1 Stat. 103)) *in toto*:

CONGRESS of the United States: AT THE SECOND SESSION,

> Begun and held, one thousand seven hundred and ninety.

An ACT to establish an uniform Rule of Naturalization.

> *Be it enacted by the SENATE and HOUSE of REPRESENTATIVES of the United States of America, in Congress assembled, That any alien,*

being a free white person, who shall have resided within the limits and under the jurisdiction of the United States for the term of two years, may be admitted to become a citizen thereof, on application to any Common Law Court of Record, in any one of the States wherein he shall have resided for the term of one year at least, and making proof to the satisfaction of such Court, that he is a person of good character, and taking the oath or affirmation prescribed by law, to support the Constitution of the United States, which oath or affirmation such Court shall administer, and the Clerk of such Court shall record such application, and the proceedings thereon; and thereupon such person shall be considered a citizen of the United States. And the children of such person so naturalized, dwelling within the United States, being under the age of twenty-one years at the time of such naturalization, shall also be considered as citizens of the United States. And the children of citizens of the United States that may be born beyond sea, or out of the limits of the United States, shall be considered as natural born citizens; Provided, That the right of citizenship shall not descend to persons whose fathers have never been resident in the United States; Provided also, That no person heretofore proscribed by any State, shall be admitted a citizen as aforesaid, except by an act of Legislature of the State in which such person was proscribed. - **Frederick August Mulenberg**, Speaker of the House of Representatives, **John Adams**, Vice President of the United States, and President of the Senate. Approved, March 26th, 1790 George Washington, President of the United States. - Harvard University-Harvard Law School Library/United States. Congress of the United States: At the second session, begun and held at the city of New York, on Monday the fourth of January, one thousand seven hundred and ninety. "An act to establish an uniform rule of naturalization." [New York: Printed by Childs and Swaine, 1790].

The history of naturalization reveals that citizenship was acquired through men. While the 1790 Act naturalized all "persons" and so included women, it also declared that *"the right of citizenship shall not descend to persons whose fathers have never been resident in the United States. . . ."* This prevented the automatic grant of citizenship to children born abroad whose mother, but not father, had resided in the United States. Citizenship was inherited exclusively through the father. Congress did not change this until 1934.

Apparently, there was no standard "oath or affirmation" prescribed for the courts to administer,[38] but it is important to note that the oath required the applicant "to support the Constitution of the United States." Nowhere within this Act is the applicant required to pledge, swear or affirm that he or she owed direct and immediate allegiance to the United States, nor is there any mention of permanent allegiance, as there is today at 8 U.S.C. § 1101(a)(22), which reads:

> **(22)** The term "national of the United States" means
>> **(A)** a citizen of the United States, or
>>
>> **(B)** a person who, though not a citizen of the United States, owes permanent allegiance to the United States.

The title of Chapter 12 is:
IMMIGRATION AND NATIONALITY.

The idea of feudal allegiance, whether termed direct, immediate, or permanent, comes straight out of the feudal law, just as Chief Justice Fuller pointed out in his dissent on page 707 of *Wong Kim Ark*: "the allegiance due was that of liegemen to their liege lord."

So, the question arises: Where did Justice Gray go wrong in his majority opinion? To answer that question, you must resort to what John taught us way back in 1992, before the IRS S.W.A.T. Team raided John's and Glenn's home, four satellite offices and effectively put them out of the teaching business.

Every individual in the world, John taught, has a relationship, however tenuous it may be, with every organized system of government throughout the world. You are either a part of that system, government or country, or you're not. For example, every Kenyan is a nonresident alien to the United States, unless, of course, they happen to be living here in the USA. Each one of us is a nonresident alien to every other country in the world. No man or woman, to use the popular phrase, is an island.

If you are a member of that country, you will fall under one of two major classes of "persons" within that country. I remember the first time John read us the definition of the word "person" from the dictionary: A person is a being, natural or artificial, to whom the law ascribes rights and duties.

So, the two major classes of persons of every country are: the governors and the governed. In England, the two classes were the sovereign (king or queen) and the subjects. Justice Gray developed his entire opinion on the basis that the citizens of this Country were in the same political class as the subjects in England. Moreover, he concluded that the rule of the common law on citizenship was based upon *jus soli*, the rule of country of birth, rather than upon *jus sanguinis*, the rule of descent or blood.

Without a wearisome repetition of details, Justice Gray overlooks the fact, perhaps inadvertently, perhaps not, that the English Parliament had long ago held that, when it came to the children of the King, that the law of the Crown of England is, and always hath been such, that the children of the Kings of England, in whatsoever parts they be born, in England or elsewhere, be able and ought to bear the inheritance after the death of their ancestors . . .

Wong Kim Ark, 169 U.S. at 668 (quoting the Statute 25 Edw. III (1350)). When it came to the sovereign of England, *jus sanguinis* was the rule of nationality, NOT *jus soli*. Only when it came to the question of the nationality of the English subjects was the common-law rule that of *jus soli* or rule of country of birth.

Numerous Supreme Court decisions prior and subsequent to *Wong Kim Ark* recognized the white citizens of this Nation as its sovereigns. The first Congress and first President of the United States restricted naturalization to any "free white person." Today's 42 U.S.C. § 1981 was first enacted as part of the Civil Rights Act of 1866 and makes a clear distinction between two classes of persons:

- All persons within the jurisdiction of the United States, and

- White citizens.

It is abundantly clear from the text of the statute itself that Congress was addressing two separate and distinct classes of persons in the Civil Rights Act of 1866 and that those "persons" who were "within the jurisdiction of the United States" were not the same as those persons who were "white citizens."

The Fourteenth Amendment limits those who come within the Citizenship Clause to those persons who are "subject to the jurisdiction thereof," limiting that Clause to those persons who are NOT "white citizens," as evidenced by the use of the same wording ("within the jurisdiction of the United States") used in the Civil Rights Act of 1866, enacted by the same members of Congress who proposed the Fourteenth Amendment.

Article V of the U.S. Constitution requires Amendments to the Constitution to be proposed by two thirds of both Houses of Congress. In the case of the Fourteenth Amendment, this was done on June 8 & 13, 1866, just weeks after enactment of the Civil Rights Act of 1866 (April 9, 1866) by the very same Congress that distinguished the two classes of persons in the very Act that provided the basis for the Citizenship Clause of the Fourteenth Amendment.

The justices on the Supreme Court in 1898 were intelligent men; they were well aware of all the facts I have laid out before you, but the majority felt that they had to make a political decision to quell the violence surrounding the Chinese citizenship question and the 10,000+ cases clogging the courts of the Land.

Perhaps they were unaware that this decision opened the floodgates of the feudal law in the United States. Prior to this decision, the Federal Government was constrained by the original Articles of the Constitution to those specific enumerated and limited powers granted to it by the Framers of the Constitution and by the succeeding Amendments thereto. The States and the People reserved to themselves all other powers. See the Ninth and Tenth Amendments to the U.S. Constitution.

Today, however, a farmer is governed by laws, rules and regulations put forth by Washington, although he cannot find a word about being governed by the Federal Government in the Constitution. Nor are there any provisions for the Federal Government to prosecute crimes, with minor exception, in the States. Yet, the Federal prisons warehouse some 200,000 inmates who committed, for the most part, no crimes enumerated within the Constitution. So, how did the Federal Government evolve from a government of limited and enumerated powers to a government of virtually unlimited reach, jurisdiction and power?

Wong Kim Ark is the controlling legal precedent by which the Fourteenth Amendment effectively burst asunder the chains of the Constitution that had previously restricted the Federal Government to those limited and enumerated powers. Washington now assumed the role of a sovereign under the auspices of the feudal law. The People were now subjects under the sovereign Federal Government via the Fourteenth Amendment and, like any sovereign, it had jurisdiction over virtually every aspect of their lives, jurisdiction that previously had been limited and enumerated by the Constitution.

As interpreted by the courts, the Fourteenth Amendment gives the Federal Government the right to govern every aspect of its subjects' lives – schools, bedroom activities, employer-employee relations, etc. Yet, no one can find any mention of such subjects under the original (pre-14th Amendment) Articles of the Constitution.

Regrettably, under the *Dred Scott* Decision, a negro of the African race was regarded by them [the English] as an **article of property**, and held, and bought and sold as such, in every one of the thirteen colonies which united in the Declaration of Independence and afterwards formed the Constitution of the United States. - *Dred Scott v. Sandford*, 60 U.S. 393, 408 (1856) (tracing the slave trade back to England) (my emphasis & bracketed words).

Now, the only humans who were regarded as "property" in England were the unfree, referred to as serfs or villeins (French) (villains – English), sometimes referred to by the Latin word *servus* (slave). In their monumental work, *The History of English Law before the Time of Edward I, vol. 1*, CHAPTER II: *The Sorts and Conditions of Men* (1898), Authors Sir Frederick Pollock and Frederic William Maitland state the following in § 3. *The Unfree*:

"In the main, then, all freemen are equal before the law. Just because this is so the line between the free and the unfree seems very sharp. And *the line between freedom and unfreedom is the line between freedom and servitude*. . . .

There are no degrees of personal unfreedom; there is no such thing as merely praedial [attached to the land, as praedial serfs] serfage. A freeman may hold in villeinage; but that is an utterly different thing; he is in no sort a serf; so far from being bound to the soil he can fling up his tenement and go whithersoever he pleases. . . . But as to the serf, not only could he be removed from one tenement, he could be placed in another; his lord might set him to work of any kind; the king's court would not interfere; for he was a *servus* and his person belonged to his lord; "*he was merely the chattel of his lord to give and sell at his pleasure.*"

> *In relation to his lord the general rule makes him rightless.* Criminal law indeed protects him in life and limb. Such protection however need not be regarded as an exception to the rule. Bracton can here fall back upon the Institutes:—*the state is concerned to see that no one shall make an ill use of his property.* Our modern statutes which prohibit cruelty to animals do not give rights to dogs and horses, and, though it is certain that the lord could be punished for killing or maiming his villein, *it is not certain that the villein or his heir could set the law in motion by means of an "appeal."* The protection afforded by criminal law seems to go no further than the preservation of life and limb. The lord may beat or imprison his serf, though of such doings we do not hear very much. - *Pollock & Maitland, supra,* at 412-415 (footnotes omitted; emphases mine).

In *A Digest of the Laws of England* (1824) by Sir John Comyns (1667-1740), the Author has a section that is titled "Goods and chattels" and noted that *"Goods and chattels are real or personal"* (citation omitted).

Under "Real" property he includes *"A villein in gross for a term of years"* (citation omitted).

Under the common law of England and, as noted with approval by the Supreme Court in the *Dred Scott* case, slaves were considered to be "real property."

Regrettably, nothing in the Fourteenth Amendment changed their status as articles of property. Rather, there was merely a change in ownership; they were now owned by the sovereign Federal Government.

If, therefore, the Fourteenth Amendment, as interpreted by the majority in *Wong Kim Ark*, brought us all completely within the jurisdiction of the United States and made us all equal in every way, then are we not all "property" of the Federal Government, are we not all "subjects" to the sovereign, are we not all "liegemen" to our "liege lord," the masters in Washington, D.C.?

If this is correct, as the courts and the government lawyers claim it is, then who are the sovereigns over us "subjects"? The sovereigns are apparently the 7,000 "princes of the realm" who rotate in and out of state and federal offices, courts and legislative thrones of government.

However, if you look behind the scenes of power, you will readily discover that those who pull the strings of government are the money-powers, the huge international conglomerates, banks, and multi-national organizations, none of which has a shred of loyalty to or concern for any one nation. They are comprised of the "great men of the earth"[39] who would make merchandise of us all.

And what is their merchandise? Naturally, it is anything that will sell, as enumerated in Revelation 18:12-13, but perhaps the most telling pieces of merchandise, for our purposes here is this: their merchandise includes *"slaves and souls of men!"* Revelation 18:13.

When John pointed this out to me, way back in 1992, I nearly fell off my chair. He then went on to say that the clause, *"for by thy sorceries were all nations deceived,"* could well mean that there would be no better way to deceive all nations than by hiding the sorceries or deceptions within the very laws of those nations.

Now, I cannot speak for any nation other than my own. However, of this much I am certain: the entire reach of the Federal

Government today is beyond that of any monarch or sovereign that has ever existed on this planet. It reaches into the lives of every American, regardless of where they may live, taxes their worldwide income, will (and has) abducted and kidnapped their own and people of other nations to bring them back to the USA to prosecute them, and the courts think nothing of the kidnapping or abduction, has God-knows-how-many "renditions" of suspected terrorists to other nations for torturing and intense interrogation, denied to many access to the courts to test their detention, and the list goes on and on. It is simply untouched by the Constitution, as originally ratified, and is far and away from the purposes and intents of our Founders. Its reach is unlimited under the Fourteenth Amendment. The Constitution is, according to words attributed to former President George W. Bush, "nothing but a piece of paper."

We have gone from freedom to slavery, from sovereigns to serfs on the great Federal Manor via the Fourteenth Amendment. All due in large measure to the treachery and deception of words by the United States Supreme Court.

~ SUMMARY ~

Have you fully grasped what has happened here? The federal government took the slaves off the Southern Plantation and put them on the Federal Plantation! Then, after everyone had been distracted during the financial commotion caused directly and intentionally by those making monetary policy at the Federal Reserve Banking System in the 20s and 30s, they simply slipped the poison pill into all the "New Deal" legislation under the guise of "necessity!" As a great American said at the time, "a noose has been put around the American people's neck and it will 'never' be taken off." **I strongly disagree with the word "*never*"**. The individual power to take off the noose of tyranny and oppression is now in your hands!

Slaves cannot OWN property – They _ARE_ PROPERTY!

Robert E. Lee wrote to President Lincoln when Lincoln had asked him to lead the Union forces against the rebellious Southern states. Lee wrote back to Lincoln, "*I cannot fight against my country.*" In those days, before the incorporation of the United States, State Citizens considered their respective State their "country."

One of our fine patriot fighters in Atlanta once told the story of driving back to Atlanta from the District of Columbia, more accurately named the District of Criminals where, upon leaving the District, he saw a road sign that read, "You are now leaving the United States."

The following quote is from one of America's greatest true "statesman", from a speech recorded in the Congressional Record, June 8, 1934. Spoken by **Congressman, Louis T. McFadden**.

> *"The "new-deal" lawyers now have no hesitancy in appearing in court and asserting that private citizens can contract away their constitutional rights.*
>
> *It has been through this method that they have broken down States lines and invaded the most private affairs of our citizens. It will be through this method, for instance, that the little retailer of the country will be driven out of business and chain-store-system control of them put into operation, just as they are attempting in England."*

(**NOTE**: A more complete quote from this speech is printed later in this this book.)

John Locke published, to my knowledge, the first idea of "*Government by Contract.*" Many of you may not know, as I did not until getting involved in these subjects, that much of Thomas Jefferson's writings were based on Locke's writings and theories. I've heard this on an audio book of his book entitled *Two Treaties On Government.*

EXACTLY what has happened is this. The War of Northern Aggression (misnamed the "Civil War") was set up by the Rothschild Brothers; one financed the North and the other financed the South. Contrary to popular revised history, that war WAS NOT fought over slavery, at least certainly not initially. Now, to say that those responsible did not have this plan in mind is another question but publicly it was initiated over taxation; the industrial North v. the agrarian South. Our taxes were Constitutional at that time and consisted of "imposts and excises," as mandated by the Constitution. The Southern planters were paying the majority of the taxes as they were doing most of the trade with England. They, therefore, were bearing most of the tax burden while the industrial North benefited by producing and selling domestically and not bearing much, if any, of the taxation burden.

This was the genesis of the War of Northern Aggression. Halfway through this horrid war, Lincoln put forth the ideas in his Emancipation Proclamation. It was at that time that the slavery issue became a public cause. It was by no accident that the opening salvos of the War of Northern Aggression were fired at Fort Sumter, South Carolina. That was one of the main ports where the taxes on Southern trade were imposed.

After the war, there were some four million former slaves, now called "freedmen," running around the countryside. As stated plainly in the language and wording of the *Slaughter-House Cases*, in most instances, they no longer had the care and protection of the former owners. They had legally been 'things,' the objects of someone's property Rights, but that condition no longer applied. They had to be given not only some form of political status but also civil status. To accomplish this, the 14th Amendment was forced through the various state legislatures. In fact, if the Southern states would not pass that piece of legislation, their legislators were run out and more "cooperative" legislators were put in their place. They also burned many important law libraries in the South whenever a State refused to pass said amendment.

As stated in the court cites listed previously, the new form of citizenship, a "citizen of the United States," was secondary and subservient to the original "citizen of a State" that had been clearly established and understood since the founding of the Republic. As you can read in both Congressman Traficant and Congressman McFadden's Congressional Record public record statements, the traitorous *de facto* Federal Reserve promoted government agents set up a system where you were allowed to "volunteer" into servitude via a second- tier citizenship originally instituted for recently freed Negro Southern slaves.

The only problem is they DID NOT disclose to you the changes in your political and civil status OR the fact that you were unable to "volunteer OUT." Therefore, access to your original God-given, constitutionally-protected original Rights and Duties, secured by the blood and treasure of your forefathers, was effectively cut off and destroyed forever. Federal citizenship first and state citizenship second, "if" you "reside" within the state.

THIS IS FRAUD!!! THIS IS TREASON!! If enough Americans will learn this information and exercise their God-given birthrights, this con game CAN BE STOPPED! That is, *IF* you want it to and have the political and patriotic will to take action and MAKE IT HAPPEN!!!! The entire process starts with you!

This has been accomplished by the Biblical lesson of lawyers hiding the knowledge from the people. They have literally stopped teaching the legal concept of "person" and "resident" in the manner they are being used in our nation's law schools. The curriculum in the nation's law schools is designed by the BAR Association (a branch of the English BAR, by the way!) the exact same way that the curriculum of medical schools are designed and mandated by the American Medical Association, an organization purchased by the Rockefeller Foundation and the Carnegie Foundation (per the late Eustace Mullins in *Murder By Injection*) in the early part of last century. They obviously prefer the "top down" method of dispensing their brand of tyranny and control!

BOTH of these two words – person and resident – can be corrected and reversed by exercising your legal option of presumptive rebuttal. In relation to the 14th Amendment, one simply needs to declare that, "I am NOT that 'person' in the first sentence of the amendment.

I receive no Rights from said amendment and therefore owe NO correlative Duty to said amendment. I am also NOT a 'resident' under the scope and purview of the 14th amendment and have NO residency that pertains to any strict political legal definition imputed into the meaning of that word. The ONLY time I ever use the term 'resident' now is in a total and complete geographical meaning ascribed to any usage of said word. In the old school of salesmanship, they teach you always to answer a question with a question. A good one here would be *"are you using the word resident with a political or geographical definition?"*

If you choose to proceed and regain your rightful political and civil status under the organic Constitution, you may wish to review, modify and adapt my original Affidavit at the back of this book to your own uses. Each individual's situation differs in life. Spouse and children must be considered, business considerations must be thought through, church and religious affiliations warrant thought, etc. Not everyone can be a front-line warrior. All must make individual choices personal to themselves.

During war, the soldier in the front depends for his success on a supply-line stretching, sometimes, tens of thousands of miles and comprised of countless individuals not actually on the front lines. There is no shame in being a quiet supporter in the background, providing such solace, comfort, aid and support as your condition in life will allow you to make. As I have repeated elsewhere herein, *"They also serve who only stand and wait!"*

The part you choose to play in this great human movement is entirely up to you, your conscience, and your family and is ultimately between you and your God! May you be guided with wisdom, as well as courage, in this endeavor to re-secure our God-given freedoms.

Here are some additional definitions and thoughts you may want to become familiar with.

Disputable presumptions are inferences of law which hold good until they are invalidated by proof or a stronger presumption. Best, *Presump.* 29; *Livingston v. Livingston*, 4 Johns, Ch. (N.Y.) 287, 8 Am. Dec. 562.

> **Presumptions of fact** are inferences as to the existence of some other fact drawn from the existence of some other fact; inferences which common sense draws from circumstances usually occurring in some cases. 3 B. & ad. 890.

> **Presumptions of law** are rules which, in certain cases, either forbid or dispense with any ulterior inquiry. 1 Greenl. Ev. Section 14. **They are either conclusive or disputable.** *Bouvier's Law Dictionary*, 1914

We covered the term "resident" in the definition section of this book. It bears a little closer examination. The term, as used in the 14th Amendment, comes from Ministerial Law. When a country sends its Ambassador to the District of Criminals, the Ambassador REMAINS under the jurisdiction of his home country. This is why, if a foreign Ambassador might commit murders, get caught smuggling contraband in diplomatic pouches, or commit some other crime, they are NEVER prosecuted in the United States. That is because, under established Ministerial Law and any treaties exchanging diplomatic personnel between countries, ONLY the home country's laws apply to those individuals by signed treaties between the two countries.

The first time the word "resident" is used in the Constitution is as the last word in the first sentence of the 14th Amendment and is taken from the Civil Rights Act of 1866. As the term "resident" is used and the legal definition imputed in the 14th Amendment, it means that anyone who falls under the term "subject to the jurisdiction thereof" is automatically under the law that prevails in the Federal United States, or, the District of Columbia, its territories and possessions and NOT primarily under the laws of that individual's State of birth.

In fact, one can 'only' be a citizen of a state under the 14th Amendment if he declares that he "resides" within it, as stated in the *Slaughter-House Cases*. Just try to get a Driver's License in any state of this country WITHOUT declaring that you are a "resident" of that state. How about all those contests on TV that declare, "Winner must be a 'legal resident.'" There are numerous other examples. At least now, hopefully, you'll be aware of these "weapons of mass enslavement" and not step into them so carelessly or by not being educated about their true legal definitions.

If you'd like further proof of my analysis, let me offer these facts. How many of you have heard the battle cry of the tax warrior, **"SHOW ME THE LAW!** Because the **I**ndividuals **R**epresenting **S**atan won't show you any "law," you think they don't have one, right? Well, you're wrong! They darn well have a law; they just don't want to show you because it would expose their entire gigantic deceitful con game! The law allegedly requiring a "citizen" to pay income tax is located in Title 26, Code of Federal Regulations, at Sections 1.1-1(a) and 1.1-1(c). Section (c) defines who is a citizen: "Every person born or naturalized in the United States and subject to its jurisdiction is a citizen." The entire rest of the code is used for determining exactly HOW MUCH you owe. Do not forget, regulations are often referred to as "little laws."

They don't want you to know which law locks you into the income tax because it would be relatively easy for many of you to then determine exactly how their system is set up and remove yourself from their oppressive jurisdiction and control.

Allow me to illustrate. Remember when we talked about "how laws are made?" When I was in the legal boxing ring with the IRS, one of my legal tutors was a guy that hammered all kinds of law into my mind. In fact, part of the firm grasp I have on things like regulations and their promulgation are concepts that he literally hammered into my mind. He had, and still has, TONS of legal information copied in books that he has put together. One of the papers he had was a simple copy of a document that showed that

Title 26, better known as the Internal Revenue Code or IRC, was passed by the House of Representatives as a House Resolution ONLY! It was NOT passed, or even voted on, by the Senate nor signed by the President. If you remember any of your Civics class information, you'll remember that the House of Representatives has **EXCLUSIVE JURISDICTION** over the District of Columbia and the territories, the Federal United States.

That could just as well be called the "Corporation of the United States" as opposed to the United States of America. So you see, the Internal Revenue Code ONLY APPLIES to federal citizens or 14th Amendment citizens who receive 'rights and duties' (actually privileges that can not only be 'given,' they can, therefore, also be 'taken away'!). If you are one of those "persons," by all means pay the man his tax, and from this time forward, don't complain!! If you DO NOT believe you are of that status and that you have been defrauded, do your research and make your own decision and declaration. The decision, now truly the consideration of an option, is finally yours!

Let me offer a strong caveat word of caution here. Not everyone will be willing to do this and confront the feared IRS. This is totally understandable. However, some of you 'warrior types' will have the initiative and want to do so. Be warned that they will NOT answer any questions about these points you raise, your newly declared status or the point of U.S. nationals being identified as "non resident aliens" at 26 U.S.C. § 7701(b)(1)(B). If you move forward and file the IRS form that correctly corresponds with that status, a 1040NR, you will receive a frivolous filing penalty that will then start accruing interest at their usurious interest rates.

When our groups started filing these correct forms, the frivolous filing penalty was $500.00. It is my understanding that the frivolous filing penalty for filing a 1040NR now levied the IRS is $5,000.00! Guess that kind of tells you that what this book is telling you is pretty correct, doesn't it?! Just the size of the penalty tells you how much they fear this information not only getting out but being applied. *The Protocols of the Learned Elders of Zion* states that when caught in a lie, the correct response is "deny, deny, deny." Since they can't confront the evidence of their treachery and deceit, the IRS tactic is "penalize, penalize, penalize!" or "intimidate, intimidate, intimidate!"

The point I would like to 'clearly' make is that, if you do plan to confront the IRS with the facts and proof of their treachery and deceit, you need to have nothing they can attach or steal from you. No property in your name, no income stream they can garnish. You almost have to have nothing left to lose. It is a sad reality that many find themselves in that exact position today anyway due to the other ruthless side of the twin pincher, the usurious fraudulent monetary system.

I know, from personal experience, that other federal agencies are much easier to deal with when a correct Affidavit is presented, but the IRS is the lynchpin of their tyranny, and they know it! They cannot afford to let sheep out of the pen! Please be aware and forewarned of their established reaction techniques, if you are going to cross swords with this ruthless gang of thieves, because that is exactly what they are. You MUST protect yourself beforehand before putting on the gloves and going into the ring with them.

I honestly think the best part of this information is informative and educational. The game that these bastards have set up must be exposed to the public. It is their deepest and darkest secret. It is how they have taken all of the righteous ideals our country was founded upon and turned them upside down. It is also how they've taken the freedom we supposedly fight and die for and turned it into a historical and established form of slavery that virtually no one understands! It is the route *From Freedom to Serf*! Their *Treachery by the Deception of Words* needs to be exposed so that they are exposed. History has shown us that, like the analogy of cockroaches, they cannot stand the light! May their little deceitful techniques and tactics come to much greater public light, knowledge and understanding so that it can never be used against any population again!

Please allow me to emphasize this point. This technique is the enemy's (some say, Satan's) deepest and darkest secret! He had to reach deep into his bag of tricks to turn America into the country it is today, and he has accomplished it virtually without anyone being able to identify how it was or is being done. EXPOSE THIS INFORMATION! It will cripple him! Even if you do not act upon it, tell others who care and explain it to them.

It is almost unbelievable how simple their plan and technique are. Our collective enslavement is due to our ignorance of their tactics and technique! Exposure is their Achilles Heel!

I fought the good fight against the IRS for almost a decade. They fought me tooth and nail. They imposed frivolous filing penalties. They disregarded deductions from when I was filing and added copious amounts of interest. They took a tax liability that may have been, at most, $2,000 and turned it into a $30,000 liability. When I finally sold the home I had lived in for 19 years they stole $35,000 at the closing. If I told you that it didn't hurt, I would be lying to you, it hurt like hell! To add insult to injury, they took an additional $5,000 and had the audacity to write me a letter telling me that they took an extra 5K for "taxes that we think you might owe in the future!" I could have probably filed an action and gotten that back, but honestly, I was so glad to be done with them that it was worth $5,000! Looking back $35,000 is a pretty darn cheap price to pay for not only the education they have given me but also the freedom I have been able to acquire. As for me writing this book and getting this information out to the public, it falls right in line with an old cliché, "they make their own worst enemies!" And I am ONE!

If you STILL have any doubts as to the validity of the information we've covered, look at the results of a Lexus/Nexus search of ALL IRS Manuals using the search criteria *"common law."* These are just several of many, many search results. I believe you'll easily get the idea.

~ CONCLUSIONS ~
1. The Danielson rule is inapplicable under these circumstances. However, the taxpayer must establish that it was not a **common law** employer of the workers in order to establish its entitlement to a FICA or FUTA refund.

2. Because section 3401(d)(1) status does not apply to a **common law** employer, it would not apply to the taxpayer unless the taxpayer was not a **common law** employer.

3. If the taxpayer was not a **common law** employer, but merely the employer under section 3401(d)(1), then it was not the employer for purposes of determining a worker's wages under sections 3121(a)(1) and 3306(b)(1), and a single wage base applies to all wages attributable to employment with the client, whether paid by the taxpayer or by the client. However, certain additional legal and procedural issues must be considered in determining whether an employment tax overpayment exists for the years at issue.

Check MATE IRS!!!

> *"The imposition of the [income] tax will corrupt the people. It will bring in its train the spy and the informer. It will necessitate a swarm of officials with inquisitorial powers. It will be a step toward centralization.... It breaks another canon of taxation in that it is expensive in its collection and cannot be fairly imposed; ... and, finally, it is contrary to the traditions and principles of republican government."*
> - **U.S. Representative Robert Adams**, January 26, 1894.

The different bodies of law that are used to govern the country from the 'top down' are all started with the word "Uniform." This word is used because they are all the same, in each state across the country. This applies to the Uniform Commercial Code (the Law Merchant), the Uniform Traffic Codes, the Uniform Building Code, etc. I know that in the Uniform Traffic Code of Georgia, there is a statement, standing alone, if I remember correctly, that states clearly and plainly that the term "resident" is a "rebuttable presumption." Being that all of our traffic codes are considered "uniform," that statement is in the uniform traffic code of your state also. All that is necessary in a court is to state clearly and unequivocally, "***I rebut that presumption***" and give the official some legally drawn and properly executed Affidavit stating that you are rebutting such a presumption.

Here's a tragic story that illustrates my point exactly. I'm sorry to say that Charles' story is, no doubt, one of thousands that reflect their treachery and deception and the lack of proper education and study by the defendant.

During my patriot years, living in Atlanta, there was a local Atlanta patriot named Charles Grey. Charles was an antique dealer and crossed swords with the IRS. They seized about a half-million dollars worth of antiques. It seems like it was one of those 'seizures' where one of the IRS agent's wife ended up with many of those antiques. Charles was a fighter and did a very, VERY good job in his preparation and defense. He was *pro se* or his own attorney. He conducted himself admirably, using subpoena powers on several sitting Federal Judges along with the District Director of the IRS in Atlanta. I do not remember which line of questioning he was pursuing, but at one point he asked the District Director from Atlanta to read a statute or regulation that was the basis of the charges brought against him – Failure to File charges, I believe. What I have a quite vivid memory of, however, was this exchange in sworn testimony examining the District Director of the local IRS.

There was something in the statute/regulation about the word "person" (of course). Charles asked him to read the statute/regulation to the jury. The District Director read the statute/regulation, looked straight at Charles and stated emphatically, "You look like a 'person' to me!" Charles did NOT know the information we have been exposed to and learned here. He had no response; the courtroom was so quiet you could literally hear Charles' heart drop. You could look over at the jury and see the impact. Needless to say, Charles spent about 18 months as a guest of Club Fed there in South Atlanta next to the old Federal prison that once housed such notorious REAL criminals as Al Capone. Of course, Capone was only a piker compared to the organized criminals we are learning about here. Now, if Charles would have known what we have covered in this book, he could have simply looked at him and stated, "I'm NOT THAT 'PERSON!' The 14th AMENDMENT OFFERS ME NO RIGHTS AND I OWE NO CORRELATIVE DUTIES! THIS REGULATION and STATUTE DOES NOT APPLY TO ME! I demand my true and correct civil and political status as a natural-born Citizen under the original Constitution of the United States of

America and not the Corporate United States." That simple statement and a legally drawn and executed Affidavit may have possibly gained Charles an entirely different result and saved him 18 months of 'no-pay vacation.' Of course, if Charles would have had a document like that initially, the course of his entire case would have no doubt been different.

Here's another timelier example, (you can see from the subject matter here when this part of this book was written). This is a big story that has been in the news lately. The story has gotten quite a bit of coverage, at least on Lou Dobbs on CNN. Two U.S. Border Guards were recently convicted of shooting an illegal alien drug smuggler in the El Paso area. The two border guards, both with exemplary records both in the military and as border patrol agents, were convicted and sentenced to terms from 7 to 20 YEARS for "violating the illegal alien drug smugglers" CIVIL RIGHTS! There is ONLY ONE WAY that the illegal alien received "civil rights," as those are under the exclusive scope and purview of the 14th Amendment! The only logical conclusion that can be drawn is that we have already been merged with Mexico in some capacity, but the American people have NOT been told. NO ONE will ask the right question, and you notice that no administration official will field any questions about the incident. I believe they are terrified that someone will ask this very question and start people questioning the situation. Are you starting to get the idea on the importance of seemingly simple words? It's my experience that even attorneys who have practiced for as long as 30 years or more DO NOT KNOW THESE CONCEPTS! You can bet that attorneys like Chertoff, Alan Chutzpah-witz from Harvard, and many other of our Zionist attorneys and judges are very, VERY well aware of these facts. They not only understand the plan but its basis and implementation. These people are traitors and accomplices to every fraud and crime that has been perpetrated under this illegal and despicable *de facto* government of the last 90+ years. They are true accomplices to a capital crime of treason. The remedy in the Constitution of the United States of America for the crime of treason is death!

Allow me to relate a story that was told to us by my Mentor, the teacher of this wonderful material that you've read in this book and that is kept hidden from us by those who occupy the seats of power.

John Benson was so dedicated to learning and understanding this material and these concepts that he moved out of his house and quit his job and lived in the warehouse of a friend's business. He slept on a mattress on the floor for 16 or more months while he did the research and reading to enable him to understand these concepts we have covered here. In fact, the only reason you are reading them here is that, for some reason, it was God's will that my path cross with that of John Benson. Even at that stage John was in bad health and his eyesight (cataracts) was so bad that reading required him to use a magnifying glass which he would hold only inches away from the pages he studied. This is the dedication that was not only required but was given without any consideration for himself. So, if any of you have ever answered someone trying to tell you about tyranny in America by saying, *"I'm only one person, what can I do?"* Listen to and study the results of John Benson's lifelong legal research. Then, please, realize that your writer has put in over half of his entire adult lifetime learning and studying these concepts so that they could be known and understood by you. This was done with the hope that you too will be motivated to seek, find and reestablish your freedom that was given to you by God and secured by the blood, property and sacred honor of our Founding Fathers. Perhaps you will become a messenger and help spread this truth and understanding. Every effort is needed to regain our freedom. When you do this, you can answer that question yourself, "What can one person do?" ...

> **_YOU_** CAN DO THIS! **_YOU_** CAN HELP TO SECURE YOUR AND YOUR POSTERITY'S LIBERTY AND FREEDOM FROM TYRANNY! **_YOU CAN DO THIS!!_** You can be - not only an example but also a teacher to others who are seeking their freedom! **_THAT_** is what "one person" can do.

Keep in mind that every group that has ever gained its rights in this Country has done so by belligerent political action: the Chinese with over 10,000 court cases; the African-Americans with their countless sit-ins, court cases and marches; women, with their ceaseless battles to obtain abortion and other rights; the gays, with their gay pride parades and battles at the polls; and the list goes on. Their battles were long, hard and relentless; ours will be no different.

The struggle for liberty throughout history has been one eternal struggle between those who arrogate to themselves more and more power until they reach the point where their word is "the law," as they see things. As they gather more and more power, as we have seen in our times, there comes a point where the People have had enough and they rise up and throw all the shackles off themselves. Many of us are old enough to have witnessed the fall of the Soviet Empire in the 1980s and 1990s. When the People have had enough and finally lose their fear of government, they sweep aside those who have oppressed them. The only question remains whether they can do it peacefully and without the bearing of arms and the shedding of blood. John and Glenn always taught, and I believe, that we can re-acquire our rights and freedoms peacefully, by education, political and legal action.

John Benson has now completed his book, *Taxation by Misrepresentation, the Truth about Taxes in Plain English*. I cannot tell you how important it is for you to read this amazing book. You will discover facts, history and law about our tax system that will blow a hole though every theory of taxation you have ever heard or read. The information in this book will, I believe, change the entire national debate on taxes.

However, it does not stop with this book on taxes. He is completing a book on the jury system in the United States. His theory, backed up by flawless research, as per usual with John, is that there are not three branches of government – Congress, the Executive and Judicial branches – but FOUR branches, the three cited here plus the Fourth, the People through their juries in all civil and criminal cases. In short, his research will show that the Founders intended the juries to act as the "circuit-breaker" on excessive governmental actions, meaning that no law, civil or criminal, was to have any force or effect upon the People unless and until the People themselves "ratified" or gave their approval to any such laws through their approval or disapproval of said laws through their juries around the Country. It is my belief that an educated populace will enable at least one juror out of twelve to nullify any criminal law that exceeds the rightful reach or jurisdiction of our Constitution. One out of twelve (1/12th) is just slightly more than 8% of the People who need to be educated as to our rights, privileges and immunities.

John used to close the weekend session on law with this illustration.

> *"You are invited to play a basketball game. You and your teammates dress up in your best basketball outfits. You've got your fancy outfits on and the nice new $150.00 sneakers that will give you every*

advantage against your opposition. When you get to the court you find that as you step out on it the surface is really slippery! You can't get your balance and the ball is hard to control. On top of that the floor is not only slippery it's darn cold! Then the other team comes out. They are not wearing basketball outfits; they have on heavier black outfits, with pads! Their $150.00 sneakers have these long blades on them that allow them to literally zip around and run circles around you. They've got sticks and their basketball is this little thing that's hard and black! It travels past you at over 100 miles per hour and it hurts when it hits you!

You see; that's been going on for decades now. Our team has been playing basketball and their team has been playing hockey! Honestly, who do you think is going to win that game? Who do you think is going to be victorious EVERY SINGLE TIME?

We've been trying to play Constitutional Law and they've been playing "contract law" with slaves that have access to NO true Rights, just government-granted privileges. I hear educated well-intentioned and well-meaning people say constantly, "they are violating my Constitutional rights!" or "this is unconstitutional!" They are playing by established rules in THEIR court, we just don't understand the game OR the rules! Slaves have "civil rights" and have NO ACCESS to the Constitution! Get this important concept through you heads folks! What is the definition of insanity? "Doing the exact same thing over and over and expecting different results!""

Could it possibly be any clearer?

Maybe now you'll internalize and understand this statement better. **"The only way I can protect MY liberty is to help you protect yours!"**

<u>*99% of Americans don't even know what liberty IS, much less that they've lost it!*</u>

~ Remedy ~
For many years I lived as a freeman in the United States. It was very strange for me in this respect. Knowing what I've come to know and understand over these last 18 plus years, I executed an Affidavit that corrected my true political status and Citizenship. I was literally a freeman living in a land of slaves who 'thought' they were free! That is one of the reasons that I included the Goethe quote in the quote section you have previously read. "There are none so helplessly enslaved as those who falsely believe they are free."

After 911, after the passage of The Patriot Act immediately following that tragedy, and after its progressive implementation in the following years, it became harder and harder for me to live any type of normal life in the country of my birth. Those situations, plus other aspects, were the prime motivations that lead me to make the decision to leave the country and move to Argentina.

During those years, I thought about the possibility that I would have some kind of confrontation with some sort of federal or State of Florida enforcement agency and have to defend my position. That situation never occurred. Nevertheless, I put quite a bit of time into visualizing such a scenario and not only what possible course I would take, but also what technique I would use. Again, I never was put in that position, so what I am going to tell you has never been tested. Not, at least, by me personally. However, the legal basis and theory is solid according to established 'black-letter law,' as it's often referred to.

Keep in mind that any time one has to address or initiate any action with government, they want you to, their words, not mine, "exhaust your administrative remedies" before taking such action to any court. That means attempting to get whatever problem you are having settled at the administrative lower level before court actions are needed or initiated.

My personal experiences doing this, to this point, have always been not only successful but also incredibly easy. I have never had any type of confrontation presenting that Affidavit. Those experiences have already been stated earlier but, due to the importance of this information, I will state them again. Using the Affidavit that I filed correctly on December 31, 1992 (reprinted at the back of this book), I have accomplished the following events with 100% success.

- First, I removed myself for being a "taxpayer" or being required to file, with the exception of reporting income received under 26 C.F.R. §§ 871(b) and 877(b). Both of those sections only pertain to constitutionally mandated taxation.

- Second, obtaining a State of Florida picture, hologram ID card through the Florida Driver's License Division, declaring myself when applying to be a "non-resident" and "non citizen of the United States."

While taking the information, the clerk scanned the Affidavit into the computer, and it was obviously being attached to my profile in their database. I used that picture ID as the fulfilling requirement to apply for my first passport.

The clerk at the Post Office required me to have a picture ID even though the instructions on the application stated you could bring someone with you that had known you for two years, which I had done.

- I received that passport. That passport was stolen in February 2010 and I had to apply through the Embassy in Buenos Aires for a replacement.

- I received that replacement passport after personally handing the Affidavit to the official from the Embassy in charge of that particular department. It was the first and only time I have ever gotten to give my Affidavit personally to a representative of the federal government. I also, in an overview, explained it to her.

- I used that passport to apply for my social security benefits, which also had to be done through the Embassy. I insisted to the official handling that application that it was to be attached to and incorporated by reference to that application. Within two months I was receiving those social security checks and still do.

Not once, not one single time, has anyone at any of those agencies or departments as much as uttered a single objection. The IRS doesn't object, they just try and bulldoze you with fines, penalties and interest. You know, their favorite trick, intimidation.

There were, I am sure, thousands of those Affidavits from John and Glenn's students sent to the IRS. Not one, NOT ONE SINGLE TIME, has one ever been objected to or, even more importantly, rebutted.

Of course, the IRS will throw monetary fines at you, but they will NEVER confront the facts or discuss the pertinent issues.

In law, and especially with Affidavits, "silence deems consent." The mere fact that none of those has been rebutted in almost 20 years should bare no further question or explanation. You are dealing not only with truth but the highest single form of truth in the entire legal system!

The scenario I had turned over in my mind so many times, just in case I did have to appear in some sort of courtroom setting, follows. As stated earlier, I never needed to put this technique into actual application, but it was the scenario I would have used if such an occasion had arisen.

One appears in a court or at an administrative agency with a copy of the properly executed, properly filed in the property records books, certified Affidavit. When called by the presiding government official (it chokes me to call them "your honor."), you state that, for the record, you are submitting this properly executed, filed and un-rebutted Affidavit. That document bypasses the Rules of Evidence so the prosecutor can have no valid objection. If you are appearing before an administrative agency, you request them to rebut your document with a correctly formed and executed Affidavit to demonstrate that yours is incorrect. At that point, the dialogue I had decided upon would go along these lines.

> "Sir, I have submitted to this court (agency) a properly executed, filed and un-rebutted Affidavit. It has been on file in the public records since December 31, 1992, as you can see from the date stamp. In law, a "person" is an entity to whom the law ascribes 'rights and duties' and which are correlative. The statute/regulation that I have been charged with violating only pertains to 'residents' (or citizens of the United States), which this Affidavit clearly, plainly and unequivocally states that I am not. Those forms of political status come exclusively and directly from the scope and preview of the 14th Amendment to the Constitution. As I receive no 'rights', civil or otherwise, from the 14th Amendment, I owe no correlative duty. Therefore, this statute/regulation that I am being held accountable to does not apply to me. I AM NOT THAT "PERSON." Thank you, sir, for your time and consideration."

At that point, my plan was to turn around and exit the courtroom. If you are detained and continue to be charged with whatever man-made law they are trying to enforce on you, the next step would be to appeal that decision. Usually, you will find much more "valid law" at the appellate level of any of our court systems.

If one is going to have to do this, I tell you, emphatically, once again. It is ultra important that you put study time into these concepts and have a firm working knowledge of the facts. You have to make this information yours! Freedom is not just about filing some piece of paper. It's about knowing timeless and immutable principles and applying them to your life and daily living. "Freedom isn't free," as the old saying correctly states.

Once again, let me reiterate. I have never had to use the above dialogue. Every single time I used that Affidavit at the administrative level, I have experienced total and complete cooperation and success. I put these thoughts here to make you think and help to make you realize and understand that if this is a path you choose to pursue, you do not do it just by throwing paper around. You do it by study, conscious thought and use of these concepts, along with the paper, to turn your life around. Your freedom from the system isn't about simply signing and filing a few pieces of paper. Your freedom IS about self- responsibility in every aspect of your life. Being free means depending on yourself to make correct decisions, and when you make the wrong ones, you suffer the consequences. That is the ONLY way that people learn. That way, when another similar situation comes up later on in your life, you have a 'cause and effect' history to refer to.

Among other things, I am a talk show junkie. One day, many years ago, while listening to Dr. Laura on her afternoon talk show, I heard her say something so profound that I've never forgotten it. In fact, it struck me so hard that I contemplated it deeply, and it honestly changed the way I think about life and how I live it. I have presented the statement to many people, many who are naturally argumentative or "devil's advocate" types. Never, and I mean, NEVER, has anyone argued the point.

Dr. Laura said, in the context of a conversation that **"we are all where we are because of choices we have made."** As I thought about her statement, it completely reinforced what I had been learning and coming to realize in my own life, as my thinking has changed over the years after being exposed to the information you have been reading.

If you reverse-engineer that statement with logic, you realize that ALL of your decisions, large and small, have consequences. The consequences of your day-to-day decisions, both large and small along the way lead up to where you are in your current life's situation, either good or bad. When one starts to contemplate that, it means that nasty little phrase 'self-responsibility' means everything. That is truly what being free is all about, being responsible for all of your decisions, enjoying the benefits for good ones and suffering hurt, pain or consequences from the bad ones.

I have come to be convinced that is the only way we learn. What government has done is made you responsible to THEM and not to yourself. Separating yourself from their system puts you on your own two feet and in charge of your own brain, which is where I think God intended us to be and how He intended us to live.

If you decide to move forward with the approach and solutions offered in this book, I trust you will keep those concepts in the front of your mind. I believe it is the way life is supposed to be lived. It is, in reality, life itself. Learning from our mistakes and successes makes us better and more solid individuals. You cannot do anything about others and their decisions, but you can affect yours. This is what their (our) predatory form of government has been designed to do, make you reliant upon them, responsible to them, if you will, and not to yourself. I have found this concept of individual, personal responsibility to be at the very core of life itself. We are meant to be at "cause" over our lives, not the "effects" of someone else's thinking and decisions.

~ General Info ~
The Roman Law. During its first 200 years, Rome was a Republic. It had a system of Law known as the *Jus Civile*. Jus = Law and Civile = Civil, or Roman Civil Law, applicable only to its citizens.

Foreigners had NO standing in the courts of the *Jus Civile*.

After 200 years, the Senate passed a statute that created another system of law for the foreigners known as the *Jus Gentium*; Jus = Law and Gentium = gentile or foreigner. It was presided over by the Praetor. He sat for one year only and then a different Praetor was appointed. The presiding Praetor would publicly state which laws he would enforce during his tenure. As a General rule, he would adopt the law of the previous Praetor, but usually they would make slight changes. Over several hundred years, however, these changes combined to become very substantial.

The main body of foreigners in Rome was comprised of foreign merchants. To contract under the *Jus Civile* was a very formal process, and if all the formality was not strictly adhered to, there would be no legal contract, that is, it was NOT legally enforceable.

Merchants did not have standing in the courts of the *Jus Civile* and were not tied to these formalities. They had, by their customs, provided for more abbreviated, easier and speedier ways of establishing an enforceable contract (just as the English adopted the Law Merchant later). As the Citizens of Rome saw the quick and easy way that the foreign merchants were able to contract and avail themselves of "self help," the Praetor, under pressure from Rome's Citizens, adopted more and more of these ways of contracting in his court for the foreigners, the *Jus Gentium*.

Under the legal FICTION that citizens of Rome were foreign merchants, the Citizens saw how easy it was for foreign merchants to contract, and they were eager to avail themselves of the merchants' legal ways of contracting. And on that legal fiction, that a Citizen of Rome was a foreign merchant, they, the Citizens, were able to utilize the Merchants' Law.

In only 200 years after adoption of these merchant processes, there was no *Jus Civile*, only the *Jus Gentium* was operative, and the Citizen had none of the Rights he had as a Citizen under the *Jus Civile*. He was just another merchant, bound by the law for the foreigner. (What is the Law Merchant? Today it is totally encompassed in the body of law called the Uniform Commercial Code!)

Do you see any similarity to our situation in the United States of America today? Do you understand why people say that our enemies know history and scripture better than we do? You better darn well know they do. But now you know what they have known, planned and practiced for no-telling-how-many decades, if not hundreds of years. Now you have tools and knowledge at your disposal to reestablish your Rightful status and the accurate knowledge to defend it as a "belligerent claimant."

From the **Declaration Of Independence**:

> *When in the course of human events, it becomes necessary for one people to dissolve the political bands which have connected them with another, and to assume among the powers of the earth, the separate and equal station to which the laws of nature and of nature's God entitle them, a decent respect to the opinions of mankind requires that they should declare the causes which impel them to the separation.*
>
> *We hold these truths to be self-evident:*
> *That all men are created equal; that they are endowed by their Creator with certain unalienable rights; that among these are life, liberty, and the*

pursuit of happiness; that, to secure these rights, governments are instituted among men, deriving their just powers from the consent of the governed; that whenever any form of government becomes destructive of these ends, it is the right of the people to alter or to abolish it, and to institute new government, laying its foundation on such principles, and organizing its powers in such form, as to them shall seem most likely to effect their safety and happiness. Prudence, indeed, will dictate that governments long established should not be changed for light and transient causes; and accordingly all experience hath shown that mankind are more disposed to suffer, while evils are sufferable than to right themselves by abolishing the forms to which they are accustomed. But when a long train of abuses and usurpations, pursuing invariably the same object, evinces a design to reduce them under absolute despotism, it is their right, it is their duty, to throw off such government, and to provide new guards for their future security. Such has been the patient sufferance of these colonies; and such is now the necessity which constrains them to alter their former systems of government. The history of the present King of Great Britain is a history of repeated injuries and usurpations, all having in direct object the establishment of an absolute tyranny over these states. To prove this, let facts be submitted to a candid world.

THIS IS EXPLICITY FOR THE TRAITOROUS *DE FACTO* AGENTS OF GOVERNMENT!

We ARE NOT "taking the law into our own hands." We are accessing the God-given Rights & Duties as spelled out and given to us by our Founding Fathers in our Founding Documents. We are doing NOTHING MORE than exposing the fraud that has been perpetrated upon us and righting the wrongs that have been executed against us as a people and as a nation. We are doing nothing more than what we are commanded to do in the above paragraphs of the founding document of our country, the Declaration of Independence, certainly one of the most important political documents written in the history of man! We are doing nothing more than executing the command given to us IN ADVANCE, at the founding of America by this document's author, Thomas Jefferson:

> *But when a long train of abuses and usurpations, pursuing invariably the same Object evinces a design to reduce them under absolute Despotism, it is their right, it is their DUTY, to throw off such Government, and to provide new Guards for their future security.*

For those of you who may not know, the Declaration of Independence is the very first document in the First Statute At Large of the United States of America. The Statutes At Large is where real genuine law is, ***NOT*** in the United States Code! It is, therefore, not only Law, but also the original law of this country!

~ Sovereignty DEMANDS responsibility! ~

You need to look no further than into our daily lives these days to discover the results of FALSE Sovereignty. We MUST NOT allow that to happen to us ever again. Notice the drifting societal heading without an established moral compass. If you are going to pursue this avenue, it should only be done with strict and established ground rules firmly in mind. If we're even going to attempt to correct the mess that these demons have made, we must approach ANY and ALL efforts with guidelines that must be adhered to. More of this will hopefully be discussed and addressed in the coming days, weeks and months. These days will NOT be easy.

The tasks ahead are monumental and even intimidating. If you are serious about leaving a country and world to your posterity that you can be proud of, your labors and efforts will be hard, long and tiring. It will require even additional personal sacrifice. However, you will do them as a truly free person. That will be your justification and your reward!

~ WHO HAS DONE THIS TO US? ~

Without getting into ethnicity let's just say that our enemies have made themselves easy to spot since 911. There has been an obvious "line in the sand" drawn by the open and patent facts from the biggest crime in modern history. Anyone who has agreed with the totally absurd government "conspiracy theory" of 911 is our enemy, no matter their ethnicity, religion (or lack thereof), color, creed, or nationality. These people need to be identified, detained or arrested and tried in a Common Law court according to established rules of procedure. That should be the first rule of business of the newly reestablished Republic of the United States of America. We have many able and knowledgeable legal minds in this area. They have already been alerted and will be ready to start proceedings to gain remedies under the processes of long established Common Law principles.

Let me say that I do not now think this is an exclusive Zionist preserve. I have, over the last several years, been exposed to and have considered our enemies' command and control structure. Allow me to offer a direct quote from a quarter that will shock or surprise many of you.

> *"From this room, Your Grace, I govern not only Paris, but China; not only China, but the whole world – and all without anyone knowing how it is done."* - Society of Jesus **Superior General**

Tambourini to the Duke de Brissac, *Constitutions of the Jesuits*, edited by Paulin, Paris (1843)

I now believe that the structure is intentionally set up to where the historically established Jewish/Zionists have been placed in the front lines for obvious reasons – their historical and traditional role. I believe that the Jesuits are in the background, hiding behind the Catholics in the same way that the Zionists hide behind innocent Jewry, the real and true Jews that are totally and completely against Zionism and the "State of Israel."

I can't say this for sure, but I will say that it's a well- thought-out and, I believe, provable thesis on their structure. I don't have a dog in the fight and I don't care where the guilty chips may fall, I just WANT THEM TO FALL!!! Please let me say this. There are many, MANY fine Jewish people out there. I've known quite a few of them from years in the music business and from retail, when I was much younger in my college days.

We DO NOT want to hurt these people, as they are as much victims as everyone else, if not more so. I say to you, REAL Jews: you MUST start policing your own ranks. The Ash Zionists have taken and are using control of your race and use the good Jews as shields for the vindictiveness of their rotten deeds. They do this purposefully to get your financial and other support, as they act like they're "helping you fight anti-Semitism." It has been totally documented that the Zionist elements have actually provoked good Jewish people by organizing and leading Nazi parades, painting swastikas on synagogues, etc. Read some of Henry Makow's articles on rense.com or at www.henrymakow.com and get background from someone who IS Jewish for more detail. Rense.com has an incredible archive of articles, many written by Jews, on Zionism.

With that I will close this somewhat lengthy booklet. I know that you've had much new and, to some of you, totally foreign thoughts, facts and concepts thrown at you as you have read through this information. That is why this was written, so that you can access this book and refer back to the facts contained therein. "Follow the bouncing ball" and regain your God-given freedoms and liberties.

We will attempt to answer questions as we move forward but please remember that our enemy is very strong and that we have been tremendously weakened over the years by his treachery. Situations will arise that could never have been anticipated. We will have to keep our heads up, work together and find the accurate answers to those questions.

That is why it is so vitally important to study this information and these concepts. You MUST "make it yours." If not, it is just another bunch of cookie-cutter information, and that is not what this struggle is all about. We will also have to address what our treacherous leaders would not face and that is the correct civil and political status of the Negro race. There are, without a doubt, many fine black Americans, NOT Afro-Americans, but simply Americans. This is a problem that has been simmering in America since its literal founding and it WILL HAVE TO BE ADDRESSED after we regain political power and control.
This and other situations have the ability to be extremely divisive. We cannot let them be used to de-rail our efforts and duty. These are things that need to be thought about and discussed in the immediate future. With all this history in mind, we cannot afford to let this situation fester and be used to divide us EVER AGAIN!

Again, thank you for purchasing and reading this material. It is my true hope and prayer that these facts and concepts will touch you deeply inside your breast as they did me over 18 years ago. Those many and, at times, difficult years have brought me to this point. I never in my wildest dreams thought that I would be writing a book, much less on these complicated issues, but it seems to be my destiny. I hope, through reading these words and studying these concepts, you will start your journey and possibly fulfill your own potential and role.

Thank you for reading. It is my hope and prayer that God will awaken the fire of liberty in your breast.

Roger S. Sayles

Please read the words of the late and truly great American Congressman Louis T. McFadden. He speaks from the grave as to the exact nature and method of the crimes perpetrated upon the American people and, through them, the people of the world.

Congressman Louis T. McFadden, one of America's greatest Representatives.

Thursday, May 4, 1933:

> Mr. McFadden. ***Mr. Chairman, the United States is bankrupt.*** *It has been bankrupted by the corrupt and dishonest Federal Reserve banks. It has repudiated its debt to its own citizens. <u>Its chief foreign creditor is Great Britain, and a British bailiff has been at the White House and British agents are in the United States Treasury making inventories and arranging terms of liquidation.</u> In close cooperation with the British bailiff a French bailiff has been standing by with a staff of experts and 25 of the leading French journalists. The 'united front' has arrived at Washington.*
>
> *Mr. Chairman, the Federal Reserve Board has offered to collect the British claims in full from the American public by trickery and corruption, if Great Britain will help it to conceal its crimes. The British are shielding their agents, the Federal Reserve System because they do not wish that system of robbery destroyed here.*
>
> *They wish it to continue for their benefit. By means of it Great Britain has become the financial mistress of the world."*

Mr. Chairman, I am well aware that the international bankers who drive up to the door of the United States Treasury in their limousines look down with scorn upon Members of Congress because we work for so little, while they draw millions a year. The difference is that we earn or try to earn what we get and they steal the greater part of their takings."

Later, on Friday, June 8th, 1934:

"And it is a startling fact, in connection with this, that most of the legal advisers, especially in key positions, are Jews. Felix Frankfurter's adept student and protégé, Jerome N. Frank, general counsel of Agricultural Adjustment Administration, delivered an address before the Association of American Law Schools, thirty-first annual meeting, at Chicago, December 30, 1933, on Experimental Jurisprudence and the New Deal. A reading of this address shows the contempt of the Frankfurter lawyers for the Constitution of the land and an expressed determination to obviate and avoid constitutional barriers in their administration of the Nation's affairs. Those in charge of the plan and its administration in the United States have for years considered methods for accomplishing their ends without regard to the Constitution of the United States.

They recognize the fact that the National Industrial Recovery Act did not give them all of the power they desired in order to break down the barriers enacted in our Constitution, preserving certain rights to the various States of the Union, as well as other features. **Therefore, in the promulgation of the various codes affecting industry and agriculture throughout the**

<u>country they have sought to compel, browbeat, and bulldoze the business interests of this country to engage in private contract so that they would have the power to require the business interests of the Nation to do their wishes regardless of the Constitution. The "new-deal" lawyers now have no hesitancy in appearing in court and asserting that private citizens can contract away their constitutional rights. It has been through this method that they have broken down States lines and invaded the most private affairs of our citizens,</u> It will be through this method, for instance, that the little retailer of the country will be driven out of business and chain-store- system control of them put into operation, just as they are attempting in England.

There is no better illustration of this group of international would-be Caesars to control the industry and agricultural interests of this Nation than that demonstrated in the methods they have employed to try to coerce and compel the Ford Motor Company to sign the automobile manufacturers' code. It should be borne in mind that even General Johnson himself has had to admit to the Comptroller General of the United States that he has no evidence of code or law violation on the part of the Ford Motor Company. It should also be borne in mind that the little Jewish Assistant Attorney General, Cahffetz, <u>who appeared in the Supreme Court of the District of Columbia</u> for the Government in recent cases brought therein by a Ford dealer, admitted to the court that he had no evidence of law violation. Therefore a question of whether or not the Ford Motor Company has violated the law or the codes is not raised. It is admitted by the Government that have they not. Then why all this stir to prevent the purchase by the Government of Ford products? There are two outstanding reasons: One is that the Ford Motor Company represents the last stronghold of independent industry in this Nation, hence it must be destroyed. It interferes with their plans. Next, so long as the Ford Motor Company, refuses to sign any code and thus engage in private contract which would give the administration power over and beyond the law it is still free at any time it chooses to attack the constitutionality of these extraordinary measures. Frankfurter lawyers contend that one who has signed the code has waived his rights to make such an attack.

Therefore the power of Government will be used to bludgeon and compel, if it can, this last stronghold of independent industry to come within the fold so that it will be safe from attack in this quarter.

The American people may feel exceedingly grateful that someone has shown some degree of patriotic sanity in this respect, and the Ford Motor Company has a great many of the smaller business enterprises of the Nation with them in the stand.

We not only see the hurried and frenzied regimentation of industry and agriculture in this Nation by means of codes, but we are also witnessing a most spectacular engagement by government in the private loan field. Billions of dollars are being used t take over debts and pledge the property of industry, farmers, and homeowners. This paves the way for the day near at hand when Government corporations will begin to take over and operate industrial enterprises and land and home organizations. We are on the threshold of a modern and Machiavellian *feudal system devised and controlled by a group of international usurpers.*

It might be well to observe that those who for 15 years have planned this specific legislation which is now operating to take over and control the most intimate affairs of our national life must have foreseen the conditions under which they could make such a plan possible. Therefore, it is reasonable to assume that they had some direct part in bringing about the conditions which make it possible to place the "plan" in operation. There has not been an administration since our advent into the great World War in which Bernard M. Baruch has not been a chief political advisor, and every administration that has listened to him has carried us deeper and deeper into financial chaos, and today we are operating on his greatest experiment – a planned economy and industrial and agricultural control. The Juggernaut has been built and it is being moved on its cumbersome wheels. It is only a matter of time until it will give its lurch and roll upon and crush those who have built it." - **Congressman Louis T. McFadden,** June 8, 1934

PERTINENT AND IMPORTANT RELATED DOCUMENTS

~ OPTIONAL IMPORTANT READING ~

~ Ten Planks Of The Communist Manifesto ~

1. Abolition of property in land and the application of all rents of land to public purposes.

2. A heavy progressive or graduated income tax.

3. Abolition of all right of inheritance

4. Confiscation of the property of all emigrants and rebels.

5. Centralization of the credit in the hands of the State, by means of a national bank with State capital and an exclusive monopoly.

6. Centralization of the means of communications and transport in the hands of the State.

7. Extension of factories and instruments of production owned by the State, the bringing into cultivation of waste lands, and the improvement of the soil generally in accordance with a common plan.

8. Equal liability of all to labor. Establishment of industrial armies especially for agriculture.

9. Combination of agriculture with manufacturing industries; gradual abolition of the distinction between town and country, by a more equitable distribution of population over the country.

10. Free education for all children in public schools.

abolition of children's factory labor in its present form. Combination of education with industrial production, etc., etc.

~ Revelation 18 ~

1. And after these things I saw another angel come down from heaven, having great power; and the earth was lightened with his glory.

2. And he cried mightily with a strong voice, saying, Babylon the great is fallen, is fallen, and is become the habitation of devils, and the hold of every foul spirit, and a cage of every unclean and hateful bird.

3. For all nations have drunk of the wine of the wrath of her fornication, and the kings of the earth have committed fornication with her, and the merchants of the earth are waxed rich through the abundance of her delicacies.

4. And I heard another voice from heaven, saying, Come out of her, my people, that ye be not partakers of her sins, and that ye receive not of her plagues.

5. For her sins have reached unto heaven, and God hath remembered her iniquities.

6. Reward her even as she rewarded you, and double unto her double according to her works: in the cup which she hath filled fill to her double.

7. How much she hath glorified herself, and lived deliciously, so much torment and sorrow give her: for she saith in her heart, I sit a queen, and am no widow, and shall see no sorrow.

8. Therefore shall her plagues come in one day, death, and mourning, and famine; and she shall be utterly burned with fire: for strong is the Lord God who judgeth her.

9. And the kings of the earth, who have committed fornication and lived deliciously with her, shall bewail her, and lament for her, when they shall see the smoke of her burning,

10. Standing afar off for the fear of her torment, saying, Alas, alas, that great city Babylon, that mighty city! for in one hour is thy judgment come.

11. And the merchants of the earth shall weep and mourn over her; for no man buyeth their merchandise any more:

12. The merchandise of gold, and silver, and precious stones, and of pearls, and fine linen, and purple, and silk, and scarlet, and all thyine wood, and all manner vessels of ivory, and all manner vessels of most precious wood, and of brass, and iron, and marble,

13. And cinnamon, and odours, and ointments, and frankincense, and wine, and oil, and fine flour, and wheat, and beasts, and sheep, and horses, and chariots, **and slaves, and souls** of men.

14. And the fruits that thy soul lusted after are departed from thee, and all things which were dainty and goodly are departed from thee, and thou shalt find them no more at all.

15. The merchants of these things, which were made rich by her, shall stand afar off for the fear of her torment, weeping and wailing,

16. And saying, Alas, alas, that great city, that was clothed in fine linen, and purple, and scarlet, and decked with gold, and precious stones, and pearls!

17. For in one hour so great riches is come to nought., and every shipmaster, and all the company in ships, and sailors, and as many as trade by sea, stood afar off,

18. And cried when they saw the smoke of her burning, saying, What city is like unto this great city!

19. And they cast dust on their heads, and cried, weeping and wailing, saying, Alas, alas, that great city, wherein were made rich all that had ships in the sea by reason of her costliness! for in one hour is she made desolate.

20. Rejoice over her, thou heaven, and ye holy apostles and prophets; for God hath avenged you on her.

21. And a mighty angel took up a stone like a great millstone, and cast it into the sea, saying, Thus with violence shall that great city Babylon be thrown down, and shall be found no more at all.

22. And the voice of harpers, and musicians, and of pipers, and trumpeters, shall be heard no more at all in thee; and no craftsman, of whatsoever craft he be, shall be found any more in thee; and the sound of a millstone shall be heard no more at all in thee;

23. And the light of a candle shall shine no more at all in thee; and the voice of the bridegroom and of the bride shall be heard no more at all in thee: **for thy merchants were the great men of the earth; for by thy sorceries were all nations deceived.**

24. And in her was found the blood of prophets, and of saints, and of all that were slain upon the earth.

This now becomes a question you must ask and answer for yourself. If Satan literally owns your body, does he also own your soul? Only you can come to a conclusion that satisfies yourself, your God and your conscience.

In CONGRESS, July 4, 1776.

The unanimous Declaration of the thirteen united States of America,

When in the Course of human events, it becomes necessary for one people to dissolve the political bands which have connected them with another, and to assume among the powers of the earth, the separate and equal station to which the Laws of Nature and of Nature's God entitle them, a decent respect to the opinions of mankind requires that they should declare the causes which impel them to the separation.

We hold these truths to be self-evident, that all men are created equal, that they are endowed by their Creator with certain unalienable Rights, that among these are Life, Liberty and the pursuit of Happiness.-

That to secure these rights, Governments are instituted among Men, deriving their just powers from the consent of the governed, --That whenever any Form of Government becomes destructive of these ends, it is the Right of the People to alter or to abolish it, and to institute new Government, laying its foundation on such principles and organizing its powers in such form, as to them shall seem most likely to effect their Safety and Happiness.

Prudence, indeed, will dictate that Governments long established should not be changed for light and transient causes; and accordingly all experience hath shewn, that mankind are more disposed to suffer, while evils are sufferable, than to right themselves by abolishing the forms to which they are accustomed. But when a long train of abuses and usurpations, pursuing invariably the same Object evinces a design to reduce them under absolute Despotism, it is their right, it is their duty, to throw off such Government, and to provide new Guards for their future security.--Such has been the patient sufferance of these Colonies; and such is now the necessity which constrains them to alter their former Systems of Government.

The history of the present King of Great Britain is a history of repeated injuries and usurpations, all having in direct object the establishment of an absolute Tyranny over these States. To prove this, let Facts be submitted to a candid world.

He has refused his Assent to Laws, the most wholesome and necessary for the public good.

He has forbidden his Governors to pass Laws of immediate and pressing importance, unless suspended in their operation till his Assent should be obtained; and when so suspended, he has utterly neglected to attend to them.

He has refused to pass other Laws for the accommodation of large districts of people, unless those people would relinquish the right of Representation in the Legislature, a right inestimable to them and formidable to tyrants only.

He has called together legislative bodies at places unusual, uncomfortable, and distant from the depository of their public Records, for the sole purpose of fatiguing them into compliance with his measures.

He has dissolved Representative Houses repeatedly, for opposing with manly firmness his invasions on the rights of the people.

He has refused for a long time, after such dissolutions, to cause others to be elected; whereby the Legislative powers, incapable of Annihilation, have returned to the People at large for their exercise; the State remaining in the mean time exposed to all the dangers of invasion from without, and convulsions within.

He has endeavoured to prevent the population – of these States; for that purpose obstructing the Laws for Naturalization of Foreigners; refusing to pass others to encourage their migrations hither, and raising the conditions of new Appropriations of Lands.

He has obstructed the Administration of Justice, by refusing his Assent to Laws for establishing Judiciary powers.

He has made Judges dependent on his Will alone, for the tenure of their offices, and the amount and payment of their salaries.

He has erected a multitude of New Offices, and sent hither swarms of Officers to harass our people, and eat out their substance.

He has kept among us, in times of peace, Standing armies without the Consent of our legislatures.

He has affected to render the Military independent of and superior to the Civil power.

He has combined with others to subject us to a jurisdiction foreign to our constitution, and unacknowledged by our laws; giving his Assent to their Acts of pretended Legislation:

For Quartering large bodies of armed troops among us:

For protecting them, by a mock Trial, from punishment for any Murders which they should commit on the Inhabitants of these States:

For cutting off our Trade with all parts of the world:

For imposing Taxes on us without our Consent:

For depriving us in many cases, of the benefits of Trial by Jury:

For transporting us beyond Seas to be tried for pretended offences

For abolishing the free System of English Laws in a neighbouring Province, establishing therein an Arbitrary government, and enlarging its Boundaries so as to render it at once an example and fit instrument for introducing the same absolute rule into these Colonies:

For taking away our Charters, abolishing our most valuable Laws, and altering fundamentally the Forms of our Governments:

For suspending our own Legislatures, and declaring themselves invested with power to legislate for us in all cases whatsoever.

He has abdicated Government here, by declaring us out of his Protection and waging War against us.

He has plundered our seas, ravaged our Coasts, burnt our towns, and destroyed the lives of our people.

He is at this time transporting large Armies of foreign Mercenaries to compleat the works of death, desolation and tyranny, already begun with circumstances of Cruelty & perfidy scarcely paralleled in the most barbarous ages, and totally unworthy the Head of a civilized nation.

He has constrained our fellow Citizens taken Captive on the high Seas to bear Arms against their Country, to become the executioners of their friends and Brethren, or to fall themselves by their Hands.

He has excited domestic insurrections amongst us, and has endeavoured to bring on the inhabitants of our frontiers, the merciless Indian Savages, whose known rule of warfare, is an undistinguished destruction of all ages, sexes and conditions.

In every stage of these Oppressions We have Petitioned for Redress in the most humble terms: Our repeated Petitions have been answered only by repeated injury. A Prince whose character is thus marked by every act which may define a Tyrant, is unfit to be the ruler of a free people.

Nor have We been wanting in attentions to our British brethren. We have warned them from time to time of attempts by their legislature to extend an unwarrantable jurisdiction over us. We have reminded them of the circumstances of our emigration and settlement here. We have appealed to their native justice and magnanimity, and we have conjured them by the ties of our common kindred to disavow these usurpations, which, would inevitably interrupt our connections and correspondence. They too have been deaf to the voice of justice and of consanguinity. We must, therefore, acquiesce in the necessity, which denounces our Separation, and hold them, as we hold the rest of mankind, Enemies in War, in Peace Friends. We, therefore, the Representatives of the united States of America, in General Congress, Assembled, appealing to the Supreme Judge of the world for the rectitude of our intentions, do, in the Name, and by Authority of the good People of these Colonies, solemnly publish and declare, That these United Colonies are, and of Right ought to be Free and Independent States; that they are Absolved from all Allegiance to the British Crown, and that all political connection between them and the State of Great Britain, is and ought to be totally dissolved; and that as Free and Independent States, they have full Power to levy War, conclude Peace, contract Alliances, establish Commerce, and to do all other Acts and Things which Independent States may of right do. And for the support of this Declaration, with a firm reliance on the protection of divine Providence, we mutually pledge to each other our Lives, our Fortunes and our sacred Honor.

The 56 signatures on the Declaration of Independence

Georgia:
Button Gwinnett
Lyman Hall
George Walton

North Carolina:
William Hooper
Joseph Hewes
John Penn

Delaware:
Caesar Rodney
George Read
Thomas McKean

South Carolina:
Edward Rutledge
Thomas Heyward, Jr.
Thomas Lynch, Jr.
Arthur Middleton

Maryland:
Samuel Chase
William Paca
Thomas Stone
Charles Carroll of Carrollton

Virginia:
George Wythe
Richard Henry Lee
Thomas Jefferson
Benjamin Harrison
Thomas Nelson, Jr.
Francis Lightfoot Lee
Carter Braxton

New Hampshire:
Matthew Thornton
Josiah Bartlett
William Whipple

Pennsylvania:
Robert Morris
Benjamin Rush
Benjamin Franklin
John Morton
George Clymer
James Smith
George Taylor
James Wilson
George Ross

New York:
William Floyd
Philip Livingston
Francis Lewis
Lewis Morris

Rhode Island:
Stephen Hopkins
William Ellery

Connecticut:
Roger Sherman
Samuel Huntington
William Williams
Oliver Wolcott

New Jersey:
Richard Stockton
John Witherspoon
Francis Hopkinson
John Hart
Abraham Clark

Massachusetts:
John Hancock
Samuel Adams
John Adams
Robert Treat Paine
Elbridge Gerry

~ Bill Of Rights ~

Amendment I
Congress shall make no law respecting an establishment of religion, or prohibiting the free exercise thereof; or abridging the freedom of speech, or of the press; or the right of the people peaceably to assemble, and to petition the Government for a redress of grievances.

Amendment II
A well regulated Militia, being necessary to the security of a free State, the right of the people to keep and bear Arms, shall not be infringed.

Amendment III
No Soldier shall, in time of peace be quartered in any house, without the consent of the Owner, nor in time of war, but in a manner to be prescribed by law.

Amendment IV
The right of the people to be secure in their persons, houses, papers, and effects, against unreasonable searches and seizures, shall not be violated, and no Warrants shall issue, but upon probable cause, supported by Oath or affirmation, and particularly describing the place to be searched, and the persons or things to be seized.

Amendment V
No person shall be held to answer for a capital, or otherwise infamous crime, unless on a presentment or indictment of a Grand Jury, except in cases arising in the land or naval forces, or in the Militia, when in actual service in time of War or public danger; nor shall any person be subject for the same offence to be twice put in jeopardy of life or limb; nor shall be compelled in any criminal case to be a witness against himself, nor be deprived of life, liberty, or property, without due process of law; nor shall

private property be taken for public use, without just compensation.

Amendment VI
In all criminal prosecutions, the accused shall enjoy the right to a speedy and public trial, by an impartial jury of the State and district wherein the crime shall have been committed, which district shall have been previously ascertained by law, and to be informed of the nature and cause of the accusation; to be confronted with the witnesses against him; to have compulsory process for obtaining witnesses in his favor, and to have the Assistance of Counsel for his defence.

Amendment VII
In suits at common law, where the value in controversy shall exceed twenty dollars, the right of trial by jury shall be preserved, and no fact tried by a jury, shall be otherwise reexamined in any Court of the United States, than according to the rules of the common law.

Amendment VIII
Excessive bail shall not be required, nor excessive fines imposed, nor cruel and unusual punishments inflicted.

Amendment IX
The enumeration in the Constitution, of certain rights, shall not be construed to deny or disparage others retained by the people.

Amendment X
The powers not delegated to the United States by the Constitution, nor prohibited by it to the States, are reserved to the States respectively, or to the people.

The Constitution Of The United States Of America
http://www.constitutioncenter.org/explore/TheU.S.Constitution/index.shtml

Woodrow Wilson:
Repudiation of "Dollar Diplomacy"

Through the initiative of President Taft in 1909, the United States was admitted to a four nation bank pool, known as the Four Power Consortium, whose aim was to aid railway construction in China. After China became a republic in 1911, it requested a $125 million loan, for which final arrangements were still being made when Woodrow Wilson became President in 1913. The American bankers in the Consortium, wishing government approval, told Wilson they would contribute their share of the loan only if he strongly desired it, as they were not enthusiastic about the financial (as opposed to the diplomatic) attractiveness of the venture. Wilson's reply to the bankers in March 1913 was seen as a repudiation of Taft's "dollar diplomacy." His opposition to the loan brought American participation in the Consortium to an end.

> *"We are informed that, at the request of the last administration, a certain group of American bankers undertook to participate in the loan now desired by the government of China (approximately $125 million).*
>
> *Our government wished American bankers to participate along with the bankers of other nations, because it desired that the goodwill of the United States toward China should be exhibited in the practical way, that American capital should have access to that great country, and that the United States should be in a position to share with the other powers any political responsibilities that might be associated with the development of the foreign relations of China in connection with her industrial and commercial enterprises.*

The present administration has been asked by this group of bankers whether it would also request them to participate in the loan. The representatives of the bankers through whom the administration was approached declared that they would continue to seek their share of the loan under the proposed agreements only if expressly requested to do so by the government. The administration has declined to make such request because it did not approve the conditions of the loan or the implications of responsibility on its own part which it was plainly told would be involved in the request.

The conditions of the loan seem to us to touch very nearly the administrative independence of China itself: and this administration does not feel that it ought, even by implication, to be a party to those conditions. The responsibility on its part which would be implied in requesting the bankers to undertake the loan might conceivably go to the length, in some unhappy contingency, or forcible interference in the financial, and even the political, affairs of that great Oriental state, just now awakening to a consciousness of its power and of its obligations to its people.

The conditions include not only the pledging of particular taxes, some of them antiquated and burdensome, to secure the loan but also the administration of those taxes by foreign agents. The responsibility on the part of our government implied in the encouragement of a loan thus secured and administered is plain enough and is obnoxious to the principles upon which the government of our people rests.

The government of the United States is not only willing but earnestly desirous of aiding the great Chinese people in every way that is consistent with their untrammeled development and its own immemorial principles.

The awakening of the people of China to a consciousness of their possibilities under free government is the most significant, if not the most momentous, event of our generation. With the movement and aspiration the American people are in profound sympathy. They certainly wish to participate, and participate very generously, in opening to the Chinese and to the use of the world the almost untouched and perhaps unrivaled resources of China.

The government of the United States is earnestly desirous of promoting the most extended and intimate trade relationships between this country and the Chinese Republic. The present administration will urge and support the legislative measure necessary to five American merchants, manufacturers, contractors, and engineers the banking and other financial facilities which they now lack, and without which they are at a serious disadvantage as compared with their industrial and commercial rivals. This is its duty. This is the main material interest of its citizens in the development of China. Our interests are those of the open door—a door of friendship and mutual advantage. This is the only door we care to enter." - **U.S. National Archives & Records Administration**, *American Journal of International Law*, Vol. VII, pp. 338-399.

~ MONEY QUOTES ~

Here are what are few important people throughout history have had to say about money & banking:

> *"Permit me to issue and control a nation's money, and I care not who makes it's laws."* - **Mayer Amschel Rothschild**

> *"We have in this country one of the most corrupt institutions the world has ever known. I refer to the Federal Reserve Board and the Federal Reserve Banks, hereinafter called the FED. They are not government institutions. They are private monopolies which prey upon the people of these United States for the benefit of themselves and their foreign customers."* - **Congressman Louis T. McFadden** (22 years Chairman, House Banking & Currency Committee)

> *"The Federal Reserve (privately owned banks) are one of the most corrupt institutions the world has ever seen."* - **Congressman Louis T. McFadden**

> *"If two parties, instead of being a bank and an individual, were an individual and an individual, they could not inflate the circulating medium by a loan transaction, for the simple reason that the lender could not lend what he didn't have, as banks can do...Only commercial banks and trust companies can lend money they manufacture by lending it."* - **Professor Irving Fisher**, Yale University, in his book, *"100% Money"*

> *"Whoever controls the volume of money in any country is absolute master of all industry and commerce"* - **President James A. Garfield**

> *"The Colonies would gladly have borne the little tax on tea and other matters had it not been that ENGLAND TOOK AWAY FROM THE COLONIES THEIR MONEY, which created unemployment and dissatisfaction."* - **Benjamin Franklin**

> *"We have stricken the (slave) shackles from four million human beings and brought all laborers to a common level, not so much by the elevation of former slaves as by practically reducing the whole working population, white and black, to a condition of serfdom. While boasting of our noble deeds, we are careful to conceal the ugly fact that <u>by our iniquitous money system we have nationalized a system of oppression which, though more refined, is no less cruel than the old system of chattel slavery.</u>"* - **Horace Greely** (emphasis added.)

> *"The few who can understand the system (check money and credits) will either be so interested in its profits, or so dependent on its favors, that there will be no opposition from that class, while on the other hand, the great body of the people mentally incapable of comprehending the tremendous advantage that capital derives from the system, will bear its burdens without complaint, and perhaps without even suspecting that the system is inimical to their interests"* - **Rothschild Brothers of London**

The ***London Times*** is said to have printed the following during the American Civil War:

> *"If that mischievous financial policy, which had its origin in the North American Republic should*

become indurated down to a fixture, then that Government will furnish its own money without cost. It will pay off debts and without a debt. It will have all the money necessary to carry on its commerce. It will become prosperous beyond precedent in the history of the civilized governments of the world. The brains and the wealth of all countries will go to North America. That government must be destroyed or it will destroy every monarchy on the globe."

On Lincoln's death **Otto von Bismark** commented:

"The death of Lincoln was a disaster for Christendom. There was no man in the United States great enough to wear his boots. I fear that foreign bankers with their craftiness and tortuous tricks will entirely control the exuberant riches of America and use it systematically to corrupt modern civilization. They will not hesitate to plunge the whole of Christendom into wars and chaos in order that the earth should become their inheritance."

"The people can and will be furnished with a currency as safe as their own Government. Money will cease to be master and become the servant of humanity. Democracy will rise superior to the money power." - **Abraham Lincoln**

"My agency in promoting the passage of the National Bank Act was the greatest financial mistake of my life. It has built up a monopoly which affects every interest in the country. It should be repealed; but before that can be accomplished, the people will be arrayed on one side and the banks on the other, in a contest such as we have never seen before in this country." - **Salmon P. Chase**

"The money power preys upon the nation in times of peace, and conspires against it in times of adversity. It is more despotic than monarchy, more insolent than autocracy, more selfish than bureaucracy. It denounces, as public enemies, all who question its methods or throw light upon its crimes." - **Abraham Lincoln**

"Under the Federal Reserve Act, panics are scientifically created; the present panic, if the first scientifically created one, worked out as we figure a mathematical problem." - **Hon. Charles A. Lindbergh, Sr.**, writing of the panic of 1920

"If Congress has the right under the Constitution to issue paper money, it was given them to be used by themselves, not to be delegated to individuals or to corporations." - **President Andrew Jackson**

"The youth who can solve the money question will do more for the world than all the professional soldiers of history."
- **Henry Ford Sr.**

"I believe that banking institutions are more dangerous to our liberties than standing armies. Already they have raised up a monied aristocracy that has set the Government at defiance. The issuing power should be taken from the banks restored to the people to whom it properly belongs." - **President Thomas Jefferson**

The proper title of the Federal Reserve Act is the Glass- Owens Act. Here is what the sponsors of the Act had to say about it.

"The only honest dollar is a dollar of stable, debt paying, purchasing power. The only honest dollar is a dollar which repays the creditor the value he lent and no more, and require the debtor to pay the value borrowed and no more." - **Senator Robert L. Owens**, (Okla.) 1913

"I had never thought the Federal Bank System would prove such a failure. The country is in a state of irretrievable bankruptcy." - **Senator Carter Glass**, June 7, 1938

"All the perplexities, confusion, and distress in America arise, not from defects in their Constitution or Confederation, not from want of honor or virtue, as much as the downright ignorance of the nature of coin, credit, and circulation." - **John Adams**

"It is well enough that people of the nation do not understand our banking and monetary system, for if they did, I believe there would be a revolution before tomorrow morning." - **Henry Ford Sr.**

"If the American people ever allow private banks to control the issue of their currency, first by inflation and then deflation, the banks and corporations that will grow up around them will deprive the people of all property until their children will wake up homeless on the continent their fathers conquered." - **Thomas Jefferson**

"The modern banking system manufactures money out of nothing. The process is perhaps the most astounding piece of sleight of hand that was ever invented." - Investments advisor **Major L. B. Angus** *"Slump Ahead in Bonds"*

"I believe that banking institutions are more dangerous to our liberties than standing armies. Already they have raised up a money aristocracy that has set the government at defiance. The issuing power (of money) should be taken from the banks, and restored to Congress and to the people, to whom it belongs." - **Abraham Lincoln**

"I see in the near future a crisis approaching that unnerves me, and causes me to tremble for the future of my country; corporations have been enthroned, an era of corruption in high places will follow, and the money power of the country will endeavor to prolong its reign by working upon the prejudices of the people, until the wealth is aggregated in a few hands, and the Republic (note, not the "Democracy") destroyed." - **Abraham Lincoln**

"Banking was conceived in iniquity and born in sin. Bankers own the earth. Take it away from them but leave them the power to create money and, with the flick of the pen, they will create enough money to buy it back again. Take this great power away from them and all great fortunes like mine will disappear and they ought to disappear, for then this would be a better and happier world to live in...But, if you want to continue to be slaves of the bankers and pay the cost of your own slavery, then let bankers continue to create money and control credit." - **Sir Joseph Stamp**, President, Bank of England

"The world is governed by far different persons than what is imagined by those not behind the scenes." - **Benjamin Disraeli**

*"The Federal Reserve Banking is nothing but a banking fraud and an unlawful crime against

Civilization. Why? Because they "create" the money made out of nothing, and our Uncle Sap Government issues their "Federal Reserve Notes" and STAMPS our Government approval with NO obligation whatever from these Federal Reserve Banks, Individual Banks or National Banks, etc." - **H.L. Birum, Sr.**, *American Mercury*, August 1957, p. 43.

"You will recall that the first act of the Marxists, who were surreptitiously infiltrated into key positions in our government in 1933, was to depreciate the dollar and deny to the American people the right of redemption because these conspirators had learned from Karl Marx that the surest way to overturn the social order was to debauch the currency. To accomplish this they installed the Laski-Keynes-Marxist monetary system of a so-called 'managed currency.'" - Honorable **John T. Wood**, *American Mercury*, May 1957, p. 145

"The only dynamite that works in this country is the dynamite of a sound idea. I think we are getting a sound idea on the money question. The people have an instinct, which tells them that something is wrong and that the wrong somehow centers in money.

Don't allow them to confuse you with the cry of "paper money." The danger of paper money is precisely the danger of gold--if you get too much it is no good.

There is just one rule for money and that is to have enough to carry all the legitimate trade that is waiting to move. Too little and too much are both bad. But enough to move trade, enough to prevent stagnation on the one hand, not enough to permit speculation on the other hand, is the proper ratio.

If our country can issue a dollar bond, it can issue a dollar bill. The element that makes the bond good, makes the bill good also. The difference between the bond and the bill is that the bond lets money brokers collect the amount of the bond and an additional 20 percent interest, whereas the currency pays nobody but those who contribute directly in some useful way.

It is absurd to say that our country can issue $30,000,000 in bonds and not $30,000,000 in currency. Both are promises to pay; but on promise fattens the usurer and the other helps the people.

It is the people who constitute the basis of government credit. Why then cannot the people have benefit of their own gilt-edge credit by receiving non-interest-bearing currency - instead of bankers receiving the benefit of the people's credit in interest- bearing bonds? If the United States Government will adopt this policy of increasing its national wealth without contributing to the interest collector--for the whole national debt is made up on interest charges--then you will see an era of progress and prosperity in this country such as could never have come otherwise." - **Thomas A. Edison**

"One of the most devastating manipulations of the Federal Reserve System occurred during the year 1920. On May 18, 1920, the Federal Reserve Board and the Federal Advisory Council met in Washington, at which time resolutions were passed, ordering the pursuance of a drastic policy of deflation for the avowed purpose of reducing prices and wages." - **Willis A. Overholser, L.L.B.**, *"The History in the United States"*

Fom the testimony of Marriner Eccles, Chairman of the Federal Reserve Board, before the House Banking and Currency Committee, Sept. 30, 1941

Congressman Patman: *"Mr. Eccles, how did you get the money to buy those two billions of government securities?"*

Eccles: *"We created it."*

Patman: *"Out of what?"*

Eccles: *"Out of the right to issue credit money."*

"Capital must protect itself in every way, through combination and through legislation. Debts must be collected and loans and mortgages foreclosed as soon as possible. When through a process of law the common people lost their homes, they will be more tractable and more easily governed by the strong arm of the law, applied by the central power of wealth, under control of leading financiers. People without homes will not quarrel with their leaders. This is well known among our principal men now engaged in forming an imperialism of capital to govern the world. By dividing the people we can get them to expend their energies in fighting over questions of no importance to us except as teachers of the common herd. Thus, by discreet action we can secure for ourselves what has been generally planned and successfully accomplished." - From *The Banker's Manifest*, for private circulation among leading bankers only. **"Civil Servants' Year Book (The Organizer)"** January 1934 & *"New American"* February 1934.

"Duke of Bedford, realizing the enormity of the sellout of the International Bankers, made the following remarks before the House of Lords on December 17, 1945, at the time the Bretton Woods proposal was before the British Government:

> *"I find that opposition to the Bretton Woods scheme, which is one of the conditions of the loan, is almost universal among people of widely different political and economic outlook...I find that the really fine and enlighted people of America are as much against Bretton Woods and all that it stands for as I am .....Then there is the very grave objection indeed that WE ARE PROPOSING TO HAND OVER THE CONTROL OF OUR ECONOMIC LIFE, in a very large measure, to a gang of representatives of Wall Street finance who are responsible to no one and are above every Government."* - **Duke of Bedford**, *American Mercury*, April 1957, p. 137

> *"In both the goldsmiths' practice and in modern banking, new money is created by offering loans to customers. A private commercial bank which has just received extra reserves from the Fed (by borrowing reserves for example) can make roughly six dollars in loans for every one dollar in reserves it obtains from the Fed. How does it get six dollars from one dollar? It simply makes book entries for its loan customers saying "you have a deposit of six dollars with us."* - Letter from **Russell L. Munk**, Assistant General Counsel (International Affairs), Department of Treasury (**NOTE:** *not* the United States Department of Treasury)

> *"If all the bank loans were paid no one would have a bank deposit and there would not be a dollar of coin or currency in circulation. This is a staggering thought.*

We are completely dependent on the commercial banks. Someone has to borrow dollar we have in circulation. If the banks create ample synthetic money we are prosperous; if not, we starve. We are absolutely without a permanent money system. When one gets a complete grasp of the picture the tragic absurdity of our hopeless position is almost incredible, but there it is. It (the banking problem) is the most important subject intelligent persons can investigate and reflect upon. It is so important that our present civilization may collapse unless it becomes widely understood and the defects remedied very soon." - **U.S. Senate document** #23, page 102, 1/24/39, Mr. Robert Hemphill, for 8 years Credit Manager of the Federal Reserve Bank of Atlanta.

The Root of Our Economic Problem:

"Rising debts and increasing bankruptcies are the result of Congress suspending the "free" coinage of metals -INTO MONEY- and switching us to bank credits as our medium of exchange. These acts converted our nation from a wealth monetary system, where people created money for society's benefit through the fruits of their labor, to a monetary system, where now ALL NEW MONEY IS LOANED INTO CIRCULATION AS AN INTEREST- BEARING DEBT. SINCE THIS SYSTEM ONLY CREATES THE PRINCIPAL AND NEVER THE INTEREST, THE DEBT IF ALWAYS GREATER THAN THE MONEY SUPPLY. This fraudulently created debt forces American citizens to borrow constantly so the system can function. Eventually, the process becomes unworkable, as society, mortgaged to the hilt, can no longer afford to borrow. This debt creates extreme stress for us as we struggle to meet impossible money obligations.

> *The results are: a constantly rising cost-of-living, layoffs, family breakdown, increased drug and alcohol use, an increase in crime and a general moral breakdown."* - **Byron Dale**, monetary expert.

Study the monetary system dear readers. Learn the things, which they don't teach in college.

> **Suggested reading:** *Secrets of the Federal Reserve* by Eustace Mullins (the only book burned in Germany since WWII), *The Creature from Jekyll Island* by G. Edward Griffin.

In closing. I would like to thank all of your who have purchased this small but powerful book. It is the product of many, many years of human toil and sacrifice. Many people who are not able to be recognized have given their literal lives to this great and timeless battle. Many more have not yet passed on to their great reward but still toil under the depravations and assaults from our mortal and traditional enemies. They are the people who have paved the way for me. They have paved the way by doing the long tedious hours of legal research that it has taken for the excerpts and facts that have been presented here to be written and known. The best way for you to honor their sacrifice is to take the baton for the runner in the third leg of the relay. It appears, here in 2011, that the light, whatever it may be, can be seen at the end of the tunnel. It is my true hope and prayer that these written words, along with any spoken words that you may have heard on a radio broadcast which led you to purchase this priceless assemblage of historical and truthful information, will fall on ears and brains that are ready for action. **This is our time!!!**

I can honestly say that ALL of the sacrifices I have made over, now, 18.5 years have been completely worth whatever pain has been experienced. There can be nothing in this world like the true freedom that I have attained. I thank God every day for the many blessings, he has bestowed upon me and for the talents given which, with this information, I have been able to develop more than at any time in my entire lifetime.

I would like to publicly thank John Benson and Glenn Ambort, two of the finest men I have ever had the pleasure of knowing. Their selfless sacrifices, including 14.5 years collectively in federal prison, have not gone unnoticed or unappreciated. Thank you both from the bottom of my free heart!

Thank you for reading. Now, is this your time for decision and action?

Sincerely,

Roger S. Sayles
U.S. sovereign-national

"To Madison, then, duties to God were superior to duties to civil authorities–the ultimate loyalty was owed to God above all. Madison did not say that duties to the Creator are precedent only to those laws specifically directed at religion, nor did he strive simply to prevent deliberate acts of persecution or discrimination. The idea that civil obligations are subordinate to religious duty is consonant with the notion that government must accommodate, where possible, those religious practices that conflict with civil law." - City of Boerne v. Flores, 521 U.S. 507, 561 (1997) (**O'Connor, J.**, dissenting).

"By the thirteenth amendment of the constitution, slavery was prohibited. The main object of the opening sentence of the fourteenth amendment was to settle the question, upon which there had been a difference of opinion throughout the country and in the court, as to the citizenship of free Negroes (Scott v Sanford, 19 How. 393): **_and to put it beyond doubt that all persons, white or black, and whether formerly slaves or not, born or naturalized in the United States, and owing no allegiance to any alien power, should be citizens of the United States, and of the state in which they reside._**" - (Slaughter-House Cases, 16 Wall. 36, 73; Strauder v. West Virginia, 100 U.S. 303, 306).

"The liberties of our Country, the freedom of our civil constitution are worth defending at all hazards: And it is our duty to defend them against all attacks. We have received them as a fair Inheritance from our worthy Ancestors: They purchased them for us with toil and danger and expence of treasure and blood; and transmitted them to us with care and diligence. It will bring an everlasting mark of infamy on the present generation, enlightened as it is, if we *should suffer them to be wrested from us by violence without a struggle; or be cheated out of them by the artifices of false and designing men. Of the latter we are in most danger at present: Let us therefore be aware of it. Let us contemplate our forefathers and posterity; and resolve to maintain the rights bequeathed to us from the former, for the sake of the latter. — Instead of sitting down satisfied with the efforts we have already made, which is the wish of our enemies, the necessity of the times, more than ever, calls for our utmost circumspection, deliberation, fortitude, and perseverance.*

Let us remember that "if we suffer tamely a lawless attack upon our liberty, we encourage it, and involve others in our doom." It is a very serious consideration, which should deeply impress our minds, that millions yet unborn may be the miserable sharers of the event." - Essay, written under the pseudonym "**Candidus**," in *The Boston Gazette* (14 October 1771), later published in *The Life and Public Services of Samuel Adams* (1865) by William Vincent Wells, p. 425.

Finally, are you free or are you a slave? Are you a part of the "agricultural capital" of the great Federal manor? Are you and you children today's villeins?

*"The ownership of a manor usually involved the lordship over villeins and the right to seize their chattels; and so when two men were litigating about a "manor," the subject of the dispute was not a bare tract of land, but a complex made up of land and of a great **part of the agricultural capital** that worked the land, **men and beasts, ploughs and carts, forks and flails**."* - **Sir Frederick Pollock**, *The History of*

English Law before the Time of Edward I. Reprint of 2nd edition, with a Select Bibliography and Notes by Professor S.F. Milsom. (Indianapolis: Liberty Fund, 2010). Vol. 2. Chapter: *Chapter IV: Ownership and Possession*

Accessed from http://oll.libertyfund.org/title/2314/219571/3516488 on 2011-09-25.

Thanks to the Fourteenth Amendment, the feudal law is alive and well in the nation that once proclaimed itself to be the Land of the Free, the Home of the Brave. Or, should it be the Land of the Serf, the Home of the Knave?

The choice is up to each one of us! As they say at the poker tables, "I'm all in!" Are you "all in" with me? None of us can do it alone!

fini...

or a new beginning?

Appendix

"[D]emocracy will soon degenerate into an anarchy, such an anarchy that every man will do what is right in his own eyes and no man's life or property or reputation or liberty will be secure, and every one of these will soon mould itself into a system of subordination of all the moral virtues and intellectual abilities, all the powers of wealth, beauty, wit and science, to the wanton pleasures, the capricious will, and the execrable cruelty of one or a very few." - **John Adams**, *An Essay on Man's Lust for Power, 1763*

AFFIDAVIT

County of __BAY__
ss
State of __FLORIDA__

** OFFICIAL RECORDS **
BK 1410 PG 808

FILE# 92-52074
BAY COUNTY, FLORIDA

I, Roger S. Sayles, being of sound mind and lawful age, do solemnly declare:

1. I was born in __FLORIDA__ State of parents who were white, who were Citizen-Principals and whose parents time out of mind were and always had been white. And as an hereditament I acquired directly and immediately the status of Citizen-Principal of said State sharing equally in its sovereignty.

2. The U.S. Supreme Court in the <u>Slaughter-House Cases</u>, among other things, stated:

It had been said by eminent Judges that no man was a citizen of the United States except as he was a citizen of one of the states composing the Union. Those, therefore, who had been born and always resided in the District of Columbia or in the territories, though within the United States, were not citizens. Whether this proposition was sound or not had never been judicially decided. But it had been held by this Court, in the celebrated *Dred Scott Cases*, only a few years before the outbreak of the Civil War, that a man of African decent, whether a slave or not, was not and could not be a citizen of a state or of the United States ... This decision ... had never been overruled; and, if it was to be accepted as a constitutional limitation to the right of citizenship, then all of the negro race who had recently been made freemen were still not only not citizens, but were incapable of becoming so by anything short of an amendment to the Constitution...

To remove this difficulty primarily ... the 1st clause of the 1st section [of the 14th Amendment] was framed ... That its main purpose was to establish the citizenship of the Negro can admit of no doubt...

The next observation [respecting the first clause]...is that the distinction between citizenship of the United States and citizenship of a state is clearly recognized and established....

A CERTIFIED TRUE COPY
HAROLD BAZZEL CLERK
OF THE CIRCUIT COURT
By: _____
Deputy Clerk

White   Page 1

** OFFICIAL RECORDS **
BK 1410 PG 609

It is quite clear, then, there is a citizenship of the United States and a citizenship of a state, which are distinct from each other and which depend upon different characteristics or circumstances in the individual....

We think this distinction and its explicit recognition in the Amendment of great weight in this argument, because the next paragraph in the same section ... speaks only of privileges and immunities of citizens of the United States, and does not speak of those of the several states....

The language is: "No state shall make or enforce any law which shall abridge the privileges or immunities of the citizens of the United States." It is a little remarkable, if this clause was intended as a protection of the citizens of a state against the legislative power of his own state, that the words "citizen of the state" should be left out when it is so carefully used, and used in contradistinction of "citizens of the United States" in the very sentence which preceded it. It is too clear for argument that the change in phraseology was adopted understandingly and with a purpose.

Of the privileges and immunities of the citizens of the United States and of the privileges and immunities of the citizens of a state ... it is only the former which are placed by this clause [the second clause of the 14th Amendment] under the protection of the Federal Constitution, and that the latter, whatever they may be, are not intended to have any additional protection by this paragraph of the Amendment.... the latter must rest for their security and protection were they have heretofore rested, for they are not embraced by this paragraph of the Amendment...

But with ... exceptions...few...the entire domain of the privileges and immunities of citizens of the state, as above defined, <u>lay within the constitutional and legislative power of the state</u>, and <u>without that of the Federal government</u>. Was it the purpose of the 14th Amendment ... to transfer the security and protection of all the civil rights which we have mentioned from the states to the Federal government? And...that Congress shall have ... the entire domain of civil rights heretofore belonging exclusively to the states? ... (emphasis added)

We are convinced that no such results were intended by the Congress which proposed these amendments, nor by the legislature of the states, which ratified them...

Having shown that the privileges and immunities relied on in the argument are those which belong to citizens of the states as such, and that they are left to the state governments ... we may hold ourselves excused from defining the privileges and immunities of citizens of the United States

White

** OFFICIAL RECORDS **
BK 1410 PG 610

which no state can abridge, until some case involving those privileges may make it necessary to do so.

Slaughter-House Cases, 83 U.S (16 Wall) 36, 21 L.Ed 394, 407-409 (1873).

3. The Supreme Court in United States v Wong Kim Ark, among other things, stated:

> Chief Justice Waite said: "'Allegiance and protection are, in this connection (that is, in relationship to citizenship) reciprocal obligations. The one is the compensation for the other, allegiance for protection, and protection for allegiance.' At common law, with the nomenclature with which the framers of the constitution were familiar, it was never doubted that all children born in a country, of parents who were its citizens, become themselves, upon their birth, citizens also...." Minor v Happersett (1874) 21 Wall 162, 166 -168....

> United States v. Wong Kim Ark, 18 S.Ct. 456, 468-469 (1898), and where there is no protection or allegiance or sovereignty there can be no claim to obedience. 4 Wheat 254....

> Id. 470, and the opening sentence of the fourteenth amendment is throughout affirmative and declaratory, intended to allay doubts and to settle controversies which had arisen, and not to impose any new restrictions on citizenship. (emphasis added)

> Id. 471, and further Mr. Justice Fuller in his dissenting opinion stated:

> At that time the theory largely obtained, as stated by Mr. Justice Story, in his Commentaries on the Constitution (section 1693), "that every citizen of a state is ipso facto a citizen of the United States."

Id. 482.

4. Based on the above considerations and my other studies and deliberations and being under no duress, coercion, promise of reward or gain, or undue influence I have of my own free will determined it is clear from the above opinions of the supreme Court that prior to the 14th Amendment a white citizen of any of the several states ipso facto, derivative and mediate of his state citizenship, was a Citizen of the United States, that is, one of the principals of the political association identified as the United States of America;

5. And as the 14th Amendment did "not ... impose any new restrictions on citizenship," all white men born in any of the several states, "of parents

who were its citizens, become them-selves, upon their birth, citizens also," and are "not intended to have any additional protection by ... the [14th] Amendment";

6. And because such a white man's citizenship was not restricted by the 14th Amendment and because he receives no protection from it, he has no reciprocal obligation to a 14th Amendment allegiance or sovereignty and owes no obedience to anyone under the 14th Amendment;

7. And indeed it is a manifest fact observed by the supreme Court that it was not any sovereignty (politically free will) within the black man, the states, or the United States that granted the citizenship established in the 14th Amendment; rather, it was the sovereignty in "the voice of the people." Slaughter-House Cases, supra, at 406;

8. And the people did not intend the 14th Amendment "as a protection of the citizen of a state against the legislative power of his own state";

9. And by my birth I am a free Citizen of the aforesaid state of my birth and derivative and mediate thereof I am also a Citizen of the United States of America as contemplated in the Constitutional Contract of 1787;

10. And that I am not a citizen of the United States as contemplated by the 14th Amendment and that I do not reside in any state with the intention of receiving from the Federal government or any other party a protection against the legislative power of that state pursuant to the authority of the 14th Amendment;

11. And, therefore, I am "nonresident" to the residency and "alien" to the citizenship of the 14th Amendment and, in the terminology of the Internal Revenue Code, I am a "nonresident alien individual" and subject to taxation imposed under Section 871 of the Code;

12. And as the tax imposed in 26 U.S.C. 1, pursuant to 26 C.F.R. 1.1-1, is on citizens and residents as contemplated by the 14th Amendment, it is not an applicable Internal Revenue Law to me, as I am neither such a citizen or resident. Rather, the tax in Section 1 is applicable to me only under the conditions enumerated in 26 U.S.C. 871(b) or by my election under 871(d), on a year by year basis.

13. And with respect to an election under 26 U.S.C. 871(d), I have never knowingly, willingly, nor with my informed consent voluntarily made such an election. Notwithstanding the fact that I may have in past years filed

** OFFICIAL RECORDS **
BK 1410 PG 612

Form 1040 U.S. Individual Income Tax Returns, such filings were done under mistake by me not knowing that such filings were and are mandated only on citizens and residents of the United States as contemplated by the 14th Amendment. Furthermore, such filings were done by me with no knowledge that such filings would, or could, be construed to constitute an election under 26 U.S.C. 871(d).

14. Furthermore, I am <u>not a resident</u> of any state under the 14th Amendment and hereby publicly disavow any contract, form, agreement, application, certificate, license, permit or other document that I or any other person may have signed expressly or by acquiescence that would grant me any privileges and thereby ascribe to me rights and duties under a substantive system of law other than that of the Constitutional Contract of 1787 for the United States and of the constitutions for the several States of the Union, exclusive of the 14th Amendment.

15. I reiterate that I have made the above determinations and this declaration under no duress, coercion, promise of reward or gain, or undue influence and of my own free will, with no mental reservation and with no intent to evade any legal duty under the laws of the United States or any of the several states.

16. I sincerely invite any person who has reason to know or believe that I am in error in my determinations and conclusions above to so inform me and to state the reason(s) they believe I am in error in writing at the location of my abode shown below.

Date: 12/31/92 With express reservation of all my rights in law, equity and all other natures of law.

Roger S. Sayles
C/O 2084 Tree Top Bend
Marietta, Georgia
America P.C 30062

SUBSCRIBED AND SWORN to before me this 31st day of December, 1992.

(SEAL)

Notary Public
My Commission Expires

White   RCD: DEC 31 1992 @ 10:25 AM   Page 5

~ Footnotes ~

[1] "An individual is a nonresident alien if such individual is neither a citizen of the United States nor a resident of the United States (within the meaning of subparagraph (A))."

[2] Lawrence H. Tribe, *Taking Text and Structure Seriously: Reflections on Free-Form Method in Constitutional Interpretation*, 108 HARV. L. REV. 1221, 1297 n.247 (1995); see also *1 LAURENCE H. TRIBE, AMERICAN CONSTITUTIONAL LAW* §§ 7.2–7.4 (3d ed. 2000).

[3] Akhil Reed Amar, *Substance and Method in the Year 2000*, 28 PEPP. L. REV. 601, 631 n.178 (2001).

[4] Leuchtenburg, William E. (1995). *The Supreme Court Reborn: The Constitutional Revolution in the Age of Roosevelt*, pp. 132-33, New York, NY: Oxford University Press. ISBN 9780195111316.

[5] White, G. Edward (2000). *The Constitution and the New Deal*, p. 81, Cambridge, MA: Harvard University Press. ISBN 9780674008311.

[6] *Leuchtenburg*, at 133

[7] McKenna, Marian C. (2002). *Franklin Roosevelt and the Great Constitutional War: The Court-packing Crisis of 1937*, p. 419, New York, NY: Fordham University Press. ISBN 9780823221547.

[8] The **Constitution of the Commonwealth of Massachusetts** is the fundamental governing document of the Commonwealth of Massachusetts. It was drafted by John Adams, Samuel Adams, and James Bowdoin during the Massachusetts Constitutional Convention between September 1 and October 30, 1779.

Following approval by town meetings, the Constitution was ratified on June 15,
1780, became effective on October 25, 1780, and remains the oldest functioning written constitution in continuous effect in the world.

[9] Thomas Rutherford's works were known to our Founders, and his *Institutes* were cited by Alexander Hamilton in *The Federalist #84* in support of the ratification of the Constitution.

[10] "The language of the Constitution cannot be interpreted safely, except where reference to common law and to British institutions as they were when the instrument was framed and adopted. The statesmen and lawyers of the convention who submitted it to the ratification of conventions of the thirteen states, were born and brought up in the atmosphere of the common law and thought and spoke in its vocabulary when they came to put their conclusions into the form of fundamental law in a compact draft, they expressed them in terms of common law, confident that they could be shortly and easily understood." — *Ex Parte Grossman*, 267 U.S. 87, 108 (1925).

[11] *United States v. Wong Kim Ark*, 169 U.S. 649, p. 650 (1898).

[12] Chinese Exclusion Act (1882).

[13] *Wong Kim Ark*, 169 U.S. at 699.

[14] *Id.* at 654.

[15] Woodworth, Marshall B. (1898). "*Who Are Citizens of the United States? Wong Kim Ark Case*". American Law Review (Review Pub. Co.) **32**: 559; Bouvier, John (1914). "*Citizen*". Bouvier's Law Dictionary and Concise Encyclopedia. **1**. p. 490

[16] *Wong Kim Ark*, 169 U.S. at 681; *Elk v. Wilkins*, 112 U.S. 94

(1884). American Indians were granted U.S. citizenship by Congress, in 1924, via the Indian Citizenship Act of 1924.

[17] Woodworth, Marshall B. (1898). *"Who Are Citizens of the United States? Wong Kim Ark Case"*. *American Law Review* (Review Pub. Co.) **32**: 560.

[18] "In the opinion of the Attorney General, the United States, in recognizing the right of expatriation, declined from the beginning to accept the view that rested the **obligation of the citizen on feudal principles**, and proceeded on the law of nations, which was in direct conflict therewith.

"And the correctness of this conclusion was specifically affirmed not many years after, when the right, as the natural and inherent right of all people and fundamental in this country, was declared by Congress in the act of July 27, 1838, 15 Stat. 223, c. 249, carried forward into sections 1999 and 2000 of the Revised Statutes, in 1874.

"It is beyond dispute that the most vital constituent of the English common law rule has always been rejected in respect of citizenship of the United States." *Wong Kim Ark*, 169 U.S. at 713-14 (Fuller, C.J., dissenting) (my emphases).

[19] *Wong Kim Ark*, 169 U.S. at 709.

[20] *Id.* at 721.

[21] *Id.* at 715.

[22] Relating to or affected by a policy whereby two groups may be segregated if they are given equal facilities and opportunities. For example, **They've divided up the physical education budget so that the girls' teams are separate but equal to the boys**. This idiom comes from a Louisiana law of 1890, upheld by the U.S.

Supreme Court in *Plessy v. Ferguson*, "requiring all railway companies carrying passengers on their trains in this state, to provide equal but separate accommodations for the white and colored races." Subsequently it was widely used to separate African-Americans from the white population through a general policy of racial segregation. In 1954, in a unanimous ruling to end school segregation, the Supreme Court finally overturned the law (in *Brown v. Board of Education*).

Read more: http://www.answers.com/topic/separate-but-equal#ixzz1WjHMNDVD

[23] "The international jurist most widely cited in the first 50 years after the Revolution was Emmerich de Vattel. 1 J. Kent, *Commentaries on American Law* 18 (1826). In 1775, Benjamin Franklin acknowledged

[24] "We hold these truths to be self-evident: That all men are created equal . . ." (opening words of the Declaration of Independence).

[25] I am not advocating the illegal use of drugs. My point is that the Federal Government doesn't even make a pretense of recognizing the will or sovereignty of the citizens of the several states. Officials at every level of the Federal Government consider that they are the *liege* lords and that we are, in their eyes, *liege* men and women, little more than serfs and villeins bound to the great Federal Manor, "owing them direct and immediate allegiance."

[26] This principle lies at the heart of the separation of powers, as Chief Justice Marshall perceived: "The difference between the departments undoubtedly is, that the legislature makes, the executive executes, and the judiciary construes the law." *Wayman*

v. *Southard*, 23 U.S. (10 Wheat.) 1, 46 (1825). Marshall was anticipated by Justice Samuel Chase in *Ware v. Hylton*, 3 U.S. (3 Dall.) 199, 223 (1796): "The people delegated power to a *Legislature*, an *Executive,* and a *Judiciary;* the *first* to make; the *second* to execute; and the *last* to declare or expound the laws" (emphasis added). Of the three branches, Hamilton assured the ratifiers, the judiciary is "next to nothing." Federalist No. 78 at 504 (Mod. Lib. ed. 1937).

[27] 1 *Selected Writings of Francis Bacon* 138 (Mod. Lib. ed. 1937). Blackstone stated, "Though in many other countries everything is left in the breast of the Judge to determine, yet with us he is only to declare and pronounce, not to make or new-model the law." 3 William Blackstone, *Commentaries on the Laws of England* 335 (1769). James Wilson, second only to Madison as an architect of the Constitution, instructed the judge to "remember, that his duty and his business is, not to make the law but to interpret and apply it." 2 James Wilson, *Works* 502 (Robert McCloskey ed. 1967).

[28] *Griswold v. Connecticut*, 381 U.S. 479, 522 (1965), dissenting opinion. In *McPherson v. Blacker*, 146 U.S. 1, 36 (1892), the Court rejected the notion that the Constitution may be "amended by judicial decision without action by the designated organs in the mode by which alone amendments can be made." See also *Hawke v. Smith*, 253 U.S. 221, 239 (1920).

[29] In the Virginia Ratification Convention, for instance, John Marshall stated that if Congress were "to go beyond the delegated powers . . . if they were to make a law not warranted by the powers enumerated, it would be considered by the judges as an infringement of the Constitution . . . They would declare it void." 3 Jonathan Elliot, *Debates in the Several State Conventions on the Adoption of the Federal Constitution* 551, 553 (1836).

[30] See *infra* Chapter 16, note 26. [Here's Professor Berger's Chapter 16, note 26: J. B. Thayer, "*The Origin and Scope of the American Doctrine of Constitutional Law*," 7 Harv. L. Rev. 129, 135 (1893); Learned Hand, *The Bill of Rights* 66, 31 (1962). That control of executive discretion lies beyond the judicial function was held in *Marbury v. Madison*, 5 U.S. (1 Cranch) 137, 169–170 (1803), and in *Decatur v. Paulding*, 39 U.S. (14 Pet.) 497, 515 (1840).]

[31] Referring to constitutional limitations on legislative power, Justice Iredell declared, "Beyond these limitations . . . their acts are void, because they are not warranted by the authority given. But within them . . . the Legislatures only exercise a discretion expressly confided to them by the constitution . . . It is a discretion no more controllable . . . by a Court . . . than a judicial determination is by them." *Ware v. Hylton*, 3 U.S. (3 Dall.) 199, 266 (1726). *South Carolina State Highway Department v. Barnwell Bros.*, 303 U.S. 177, 190–191 (1938), per Stone, J., *Champion v. Ames*, 188 U.S. 321, 363 (1902): "if what Congress does is within the limits of its power, and is simply unwise or injurious, the remedy is that suggested by Chief Justice Marshall in *Gibbons v. Ogden*," i.e., look to the people at elections.

[32] 1 Blackstone's *Commentaries*, 40. (My footnote).

[33] One of the first six justices of the Supreme Court of the United States and Professor of Law in the College of Philadelphia. (My footnote).

[34] I feel Justice Wilson's words on this subject in *Chisholm* to be so important as to warrant extended quotation:

"*The law, says Sir William Blackstone, ascribes to the King the attribute of sovereignty: he is sovereign and independent within his own dominions; and owes no kind of subjection to any other potentate upon earth. Hence it is that no suit or action can be brought against the King, even in civil matters; because no Court can have jurisdiction over him: for all jurisdiction* *implies superiority of power." This last position is only a branch of a much more extensive principle, on which **a plan of systematic despotism has been lately formed in England, and prosecuted with unwearied assiduity and care**. Of this plan the author of the Commentaries was, if not the introducer, at least the great supporter. He has been followed in it by writers later and less known; and his doctrines have, both on the other and this side of the Atlantic, been implicitly and generally received by those, who neither examined their principles nor their consequences. **The principle is, that all human law must be prescribed by a superior**. This principle I mean not now to examine. Suffice it, at present to say, that another principle, very different in its nature and operations, forms, in my judgment, the basis of sound and genuine jurisprudence; laws derived from the pure source of equality and justice must be founded on the CONSENT of those whose obedience they require. The sovereign, when traced to his source, must be found in the man."* Chisholm, 2 U.S. at 458 (Wilson, Justice, concurring) (citing Blackstone's *Commentaries*, 1 Com. 241, 242) (emphases mine).

[35] *Murray's Lessee*, a tax case, was the first case in which the Supreme Court was called upon to interpret the Due Process Clause of the Fifth Amendment to the U.S. Constitution.

[36] The true bond which connects the child with the body politic is not the matter of an inanimate piece of land, but the moral relations of his parentage. . . . The place of birth produces no change in the rule that **children follow the condition of their fathers, for it is not naturally the place of birth that gives rights, but extraction**.

[37] "The rule was the outcome of the connection in feudalism between the individual and the soil on which he lived, and the allegiance due was that of liegemen to their liege lord." *Id.* At 707 (Fuller, C.J., dissenting).

[38] See the Department of Homeland Security website for the history of the oath required for naturalization. http://www.uscis.gov/portal/site/uscis/menuitem.

[39] ". . . for thy merchants were the great men of the earth; for by thy sorceries were all nations deceived." Revelation 18:23.

Roger S. Sayles

Roger Sayles was born in Panama City, Florida in July of 1948. Born into a military family as his Father was an Air Force Officer. Born into that style of living he was moved frequently as he was growing up living in Florida, Texas several times, where his Father graduated from the University of Texas. Then to New Mexico for a tour before moving to Anchorage, Alaska from 1962-66 where he graduated from West Anchorage High School.

His Father's last assignment was in Alexandria, Louisiana which got him enrolled in the LSU system for several years of what turned out to be his college experience.'

Roger's radio career began in 1971 working at WDLP in Panama City, Florida. After four years of being a radio announcer and music director for the station he was able to finally secure a job working for a major record label, Mercury Records, in Atlanta, Georgia in 1974. For almost 10 years Roger worked for major record labels such as Mercury, ABC Records, Infinity Records and some Independent promotion for whoever was willing to pay his company to promote their records and bands. Basically his job during those years was calling on major and medium sized radio stations to try to establish relationships with key people at the station to assist in getting radio airplay to expose records.

After retiring from active record business participation he was hired by the Art Institute of Atlanta to teach record business subjects in their then existing Record Business Curriculum. He held a teaching position at AIA for 10 years finishing when the music curriculum was disbanded.

During his teaching years he had started being involved in several MLM companies, a pursuit he continued for about 10 years. Because of his radio and teaching background he was usually one of the public speakers at any weekly meetings for presentations.

It was during the early years of this period that he was given his first video tape on taxation and subsequently met John Benson and Glenn Ambort, (the author and editor of *Taxation By Misrepresentation*) two men who changed Roger's life and set him up for a life of truth and revelation which has led to the publication of **From Sovereign to Serf Government by the Treachery and Deception of Words**.

Since July of 2008 Roger has called San Rafael, Mendoza, Argentina his home. "*I find it to be a wonderful part of the world I had no idea even existed. Lovely place to live,*" he has said.

"*The powers of financial capitalism had another far reaching aim, nothing less than to create a world system of financial control in private hands able to dominate the political system of each country and the economy of the world as a whole. This system was to be controlled in a feudalist fashion by the central banks of the world acting in concert, by secret agreements, arrived at in frequent private meetings and conferences. The apex of the system was the Bank for International Settlements in Basle, Switzerland, a private bank owned and controlled by the worlds' central banks which were themselves private corporations. The growth of financial capitalism made possible a centralization of world economic control and use of this power for the direct benefit of financiers and the indirect injury of all other economic groups.*" - *Tragedy and Hope: A History of The World in Our Time* (Macmillan Company, 1966,) **Professor Carroll Quigley** of Georgetown University, highly esteemed by his former student, William Jefferson Blythe Clinton.

Made in the USA
Lexington, KY
23 February 2014